Dutch Soccer Secrets

For both my sons Nils and Jens, and my wife Isabel,
who allowed me to have "so much free time" to write this book.
God bless my deceased father Egon, my mother Elisabeth,
and my uncle Hans te Poel who recently passed away
for the many fruitful discussions and arguments we had
about national and international pro soccer.

Hans-Dieter te Poel

———————

Dit boek draag ik op aan duits-nederlandse ouders
En aan Opa en Oma Verhoef!

Peter Hyballa

———————

Thanks to my friend, Peter!
Thanks to my friend, Hans-Dieter

Peter Hyballa & Hans-Dieter te Poel

Dutch Soccer Secrets

Playing and Coaching Philosophy – Coaching – Tactics – Technique

Meyer & Meyer Sport

Original title: Mythos Niederländischer Nachwuchsfußball
© Meyer & Meyer Verlag, 2011

Translated by Heather Ross

British Library Cataloguing in Publication Data
A catalogue record for this book is available from the British Library

Dutch Soccer Secrets
Peter Hyballa/Hans-Dieter te Poel
Maidenhead: Meyer & Meyer Sport (UK) Ltd., 2012
ISBN: 978-1-84126-327-4

© 2012 by Meyer & Meyer Sport (UK) Ltd.
Auckland, Beirut, Budapest, Cairo, Cape Town, Dubai, Indianapolis,
Kindberg, Maidenhead, Sydney, Olten, Singapore, Tehran, Toronto
Member of the World
Sport Publishers' Association (WSPA)
www.w-s-p-a.org
Printed by: B.O.S.S Druck und Medien GmbH
ISBN: 978-1-84126-327-4
E-Mail: info@m-m-sports.com
www.m-m-sports.com

Contents

---

1   In the Netherlands, the verb *kaatsen* has a general meaning of "hitting the ball." However, in Dutch playing and training practice, *Kaatsern* has a specific meaning referring to the technique of "one touch" ball contact in all possible directions of play and is linked to searching for new running positions. For this reason, the term is retained throughout the book.

Foreword

I am delighted to be asked to write the foreword for this very interesting book about various visions & strategies of developing young players. In my search to become the coach that I am at this present moment I have asked myself the following questions a lot. Why do I, as a coach, do the things that I do? Why do I train young players the way I do? And is this the right way? Why do I train youth players, and senior players in a different way? What is right? Where lies the truth? What is the truth? Plenty of questions to think about. Plenty of questions that set me out on a journey to discover what in my opinion are important key factors when it comes to identifying talent, developing potential and building successful teams.

Looking back on my road to discovery I can truly say that I can identify myself with every level in football. In my 30 year long coaching career I have worked at all levels in football. From the lowest Amateur teams to the highest and one of the most successful professional teams in the world, Manchester United. I have worked with U-7 and U-8 age groups all the way up to U-18's. I have worked with boys & girls alike of moderate levels all the way up to young talented internationals to the top professionals of Manchester United with the likes of Paul Scholes, Ryan Giggs and Cristiano Ronaldo to mention just a few. This work along the spectrum of football has enabled me to create the strong beliefs that I hold about identifying talent, developing potential and building successful teams.

Football is the most popular sport in the world, played in all corners of the globe. Culture and history have always played an important part in the popularity of football all over the world. Many changes have taken place in the last 30 to 40 years. Ranging from the physical, tactical, mental and technical aspects. Teams at the highest levels are fitter then ever and tactically better drilled. However, the same aspect that has made the difference over so many years is still in tact. It is still the players who possess the skills to be unpredictable in attacking play that make the difference for the team and the result. That was the case when players like Pele, Beckenbauer, Best, Cruyff and Eusebio were playing, and is still the case now. Look at players like Messi, Ronaldo, Xavi and Giggs. Developing technical skilful players who are able to dominate their opponent as well as being unpredictable in forward play: That to me is the core and heartbeat of my beliefs and philosophy in identifying talent, developing potential and building successful teams.

The answers to my questions about developing the new generation of young players lies in my opinion in analyzing the best teams and players in the world. They are the best because they make or have made the difference. In my search I spend many hours analyzing the qualities of the best teams of past and present. I also spent many hours trying to identify the qualities of the best players, past and present. Looking at the best defenders, midfield players and attacking players, I have identified the key qualities of successful teams and key qualities of world class players.

This information has formed the base and guidelines for my beliefs and philosophy that I have with regards to identifying talent, developing potential and building successful teams.

Kids of the modern era can't or don't play in the street or park as much. They grow up in a very fast and ever changing environment dominated by technology. Kids spend many hours in front of the TV playing the Wii, play station or Xbox live. Their eye-hand co-ordination is unbelievable, however their physical development stagnates.

Even more so that we all have an obligation to our current and next generation of young footballers that we provide them with the best possible environment and training methods, so they can enjoy the game and maybe become a future professional player that can meet de demands of the modern game.

Enjoy reading the various and different insights of all the professional people that have contributed to this interesting book. I hope it will help you on your journey to become the coach that you want to be with the beliefs that are YOURS!

Let's go and coach these kids!

René Meulensteen
First Team Coach
Manchester United

Authors' Foreword

The inspiration for writing our book *Dutch Soccer Secrets* is easy to identify: take two "soccer-mad" German soccer coaches, one raised in Westphalia (Germany) with a Dutch name and the other also raised in Westphalia with Dutch roots, both of whom are crazy about technique-oriented, creative and offensive soccer and who eagerly learn about and reflect critically on the ideal concept of our game that is afforded by an outstanding breeding ground of soccer talent.

But what are the secrets of attractive and effective youth development in soccer? Is there a kind of international, universally successful soccer playing, training and coaching philosophy? The answer is simple: what the soccer world has been raving about for decades is the Ajax model (and after the 2010 World Cup, the "offshoot" La Masia at FC Barcelona) and their Dutch soccer secrets.

Since David Winner's book *Brilliant Orange*, we know that there is an "...idea of Dutch soccer..." (2008, 13). "Then, in 1999, I finally got the chance to live in Amsterdam – the city of Ajax, the heart and soul of total soccer – and look at Dutch soccer and the culture that produced it. I concentrated on the subjects that mystified and fascinated me – the stuff that had always seemed just out of reach. As a teenager, I'd been close enough to the great Ajax and the great Dutch team to become transfixed, but I wasn't close enough to see them. Essentially, I'd missed the whole thing because I never saw them in person. When I started talking to former players and coaches, it quickly transpired that they were still out of reach" (ibid, 17).

In 2010, under Dutch coach Louis van Gaal and with Dutch national team players van Bommel and Robben, FC Bayern Munich were German champions and Cup winners, Champions League finalists, Louis van Gaal was Coach of the Year, Arjen Robben was Player of the Year in Germany, and the Dutch national team were World Cup runners-up in South Africa! The authors could never have dreamt of these facts before they started studying this subject.

So, to cut to the chase, what is the secret of Dutch soccer? This book is an initial attempt to answer the question.

In the jargon of our sport, it wasn't the result of a 2:0 score, but instead is the product of the hard work of coaches Hyballa and te Poel over the last few years, ably supported by the 18 collaborating Dutch interviewees, Frank Wormuth (Head of DFB soccer coach's education at the Hennes-Weisweiler Academy), graphic artist/designer David Siebers, the DFB high performance center player Jens te Poel and the proactive and extremely innovative Meyer & Meyer Sport, the specialist sports publisher. The authors are extremely grateful to all members of the team.

In this collaborative process that is typical of all good teams, after collecting qualitative data, the authors quite deliberately eschewed the assessment of data in the form of qualitative category formation and a scrutinizing, research methodical procedure: the expertise of very experienced Dutch soccer experts in theory and practice should at first be presented in a subject-specific way without further comment to enable the readers to freely form their own opinions. This "stab pass" into "free space" should be "taken" and "converted." Enjoy!

Brief summaries in italics are included to allow the reader to read the book from any point.

In addition, the authors also stay "close to the man" in the description and explanation of the numerous training practice forms, i.e., to coin a soccer-specific phrase, as close as possible to typical Dutch terms used by coaches on the training and match pitch. We therefore hope that the key points of each game and exercise form can be graphically clarified for coaches and teachers without the need for further explanation.

Unfortunately, there is not space in this book to discuss the currently (and increasingly) important collaboration of schools, colleges and vocational education in the development of young talent.

Thanks also go to colleagues Franz-Josef Reckels (BDFL-Westfalen), Richard Saller, the sports scientist and sports pedagogue Dr. D. Memmert (DSHS Cologne), Dr. K. Roth (Heidelberg) and Dr. R. Naul (Essen-Duisburg and spokesman of the German Association of Sports Science Soccer Commission), the Federal Institute of Sports Science and the KNVB for the many deep insights into course details, coaching and training plans, procedural specifics, game concepts and German-Dutch friendships.

In an interview with *Kicker* (2010, ps 6-8), Arjen Robben and Louis van Gaal noted a change in relationships between Germany and the Netherlands. On the subject of rivalry, Robben commented, "It is there, but I think it has lessened. Germany and the Netherlands were eternal rivals. I like the German people a lot. I like living here. In the World Cup, the Dutch are usually glad when the Germans are eliminated. This time they hoped that we would meet in the final. We are also very similar" (Smentek & Salomon, 2010, p 7).

The authors hope for a profound, creative and respectful collaboration based on their "werkboek": may the many talented young soccer "seedlings" grow in "nutrient-rich soil" and flourish for the benefit of youth soccer. We can all become more inquisitive, better and more understanding every day and all over the world.

Peter Hyballa and Hans-Dieter te Poel, DFB Soccer Coaches

1   Following the "Treasure Map" of the 2010 World Cup Runners-up

> "The best way to teach soccer to children is to play with them, not tell them what they shouldn't do."
>
> Johan Cruyff (2002, p 25)

Underlying this quote from perhaps the greatest Dutch soccer player, Johan Cruyff, is an important and, as we shall see, also widespread approach to Dutch talent development, which involves accompanying and not patronizing young players throughout their soccer education. This book documents and analyzes how the accompaniment of children and young people is implemented and put into practice in the sport of the 2010 World Cup runners-up.

Particular focus is placed on sports pedagogy, didactics and methodology, as well as training science and kinesiology, although there will also be insights into the way the KNBV (Dutch Royal Football Association), with its regional associations and clubs, approaches talent development.

The most effective youth work in soccer is a topic that is discussed regularly. After World and European Cup tournaments, a particular talent development concept is always held up as an example (e.g., the DFB coaching concept in 2009). We also examine sports science research into the effectiveness of French, Italian, German or Dutch youth soccer coaching systems, as well as German Football League (DFL) evaluation concepts for the purpose of certifying the professional league youth high performance centers.

When they decided to write about *Dutch Soccer Secrets*, the authors' main question was how a nation of around 16 million inhabitants (compared to around 80 million in Germany and 280 million in the USA) and around 1.2 million active soccer players (compared to around six million in Germany) can regularly provide:

- *World class players* (e.g., Cruyff, van Hanagem, Haan, van Basten, Rijkaard, R. Koeman, F. de Boer, Davids, Bergkamp, van Nistelrooy, van der Sar, van Bommel, Robben, van Bronckhorst, van der Vaart, de Jong, Sneijder, Heitinga, Mathijsen, Kuyt, van Persie)
- *World Class coaches* (e.g., Michels, Cruyff, Haan, van Basten, van Gaal, Beenhaker, Advocaat, Hiddink, Adriaanse, de Haan, R. Koeman, Rijkaard, Stevens, Rütten, van Marwijk)
- A *national team* that managed to end up as current World Cup runner-up after 120 minutes of play in South Africa.

World-class German players and coaches like Jürgen Klinsman and Rudi Völler and the Sports Director of German national league club FC St. Pauli, Helmut Schulte (formerly Youth Soccer Director at FC Schalke 04) ask themselves the same question, and are great admirers of the Dutch playing and coaching culture:

- "I find it really admirable that such a small country that for a long time has not had so many youth players as, for example, the DFB, has been at the forefront of world soccer since the days of Cruyff and Haan" (Klinsmann quoted in Hägele, 1996, p 54).

- "The Dutch have been playing the best soccer for years" (Völler quoted in Coenen, 1998, p 35).

- "Our Dutch neighbors have produced a good youth development program and FC Schalke 04 is delighted to use it as an example" (Schulte quoted in Reviersport, 2003, p 125).

Based on the authors' own experience as top youth players and coaches, and the extensive analysis of Dutch and German literature and interviews, this book tries as it were to "bare the roots" of the expertise of the internationally highly rated Dutch soccer coaching in theory and practice (Flick, 1999; Hyballa, 1999, p 4; Kormelink, 2000, p 69; Pabst, 2001, p 38; Leerkes, 2003, p 56).

- What lies behind the methods and contents of the Dutch Soccer School (Secrets and Mythos) (Heflik, 1997, p 45; Kormelink, 2000, p 69; ibid, 2002, p 34)?

- Is there such a thing as a "Dutch Youth High Performance Philosophy?"

- "What is the secret of the Netherlands' success?" (Hyballa, 2001, p 4).

The book proper starts in Chapter 2, under the heading "State of the Art," which contains a presentation of the latest literature and research that should indicate the tools with which the issue can be identified and discussed. To this end, the authors have read, analyzed and assessed books, technical magazines, material from the Internet and coaching videos and supplemented them with interviews with experts on Dutch soccer (Chapters 6, 7, 9 and 10)[2].

Chapter 3 describes the Dutch perspective on soccer talent in general and talent spotting in particular.

---

2   When translating terms, the authors refer to valid and reliable lexical and direct questioning by the authors.

Chapter 4 analyzes the KNVB with its ideas and conceptions relating to youth soccer development. The "master plan" (Chapter 4.1) is examined in detail in this context because it directly influences the composition and coaching of training groups in Dutch talent scouting.

Chapter 5 discusses in depth the role of youth coaches in the Netherlands. Youth coaches have a very high status in the Dutch coaching concept both in the Association and in the clubs. The acquisition of communication skills both on and off the pitch receives particular emphasis in Dutch youth coaching ("Coaching, Team Building and Leadership Style," Chapter 5.2). The training of youth coaches and the newly formed KNVB soccer academies are examined more closely in sections 5.3 and 5.4.

Is there one single Dutch playing and coaching philosophy? The authors ask the KNVB and other nationally and internationally active Dutch players this question in Chapter 6.

Chapter 7 deals with game-oriented technique coaching (Chapter 7.1), the initiation, consolidation and variation of basic movement sequences according to the Coerver and René-Meulensteen methods (Chapter 7.3 and 7.4), as well as the Dutch goalkeeping school with the libero (sweeper) (Chapter 7.5).

Chapter 8 deals with the skills in tactics training that are implemented in the typical 1-4-3-3 system favored by the Dutch and position-specific tactics training with the aid of numerous illustrative training games.

Chapter 9 analyzes the great importance given to conditioning as a performance-limiting factor in soccer, which is very important in modern soccer.

In Chapter 10, we present the youth development of Dutch record champions Ajax Amsterdam and how it is currently evolving. Third parties often describe it as being an example for worldwide youth performance development in soccer. "All roads lead to Amsterdam. Everyone is trying to get on the Ajax bandwagon: the way youngsters are coached, the way soccer is played now – Ajax is always the example to follow" (Hägele, 1996, p 54).

Is the tradition of Dutch Total Soccer sustainable in the tension between the desire to play attractive soccer and winning matches? Are there ways of empirically identifying the exact key features of the Dutch playing and coaching philosophy through further studies? The authors address these and other questions in Chapter 11.

2   State of the Art

"Everything you know about is easy."
(Johan Cruyff, *Nieuwe Revu*, February 1995, quoted in Barend & van Dorp, 2006, p 194)

In order to be able to identify the current status of the theory and practice of Dutch youth soccer development, we draw on selected German, English and Dutch sources going back about 20 years. This extensive research is supplemented with narrative and illustrative interviews with selected Dutch soccer experts. Analyses of all available KNVB videos and DVDs, and observation of many playing and training sessions at the KNVB and at clubs in the Dutch national soccer league (Chapters 3, 5, 6 and 10, etc) support these qualitative studies. Through discussions with the youth coordinators of many leading Dutch clubs, such as René Hake of Twente Enschede, Olde Riekerink of Ajax Amsterdam, Iddo Roscher of NEC Nijmegen, Henk Heising of SC Heerenveen, Edward Sturing of Vitesse Arnheim and Danny Blind of Ajax Amsterdam, the authors have been able to gain deep insight into youth development work as currently practiced in the Netherlands. Consequently, quotes on the Dutch philosophy of soccer resulting from these interviews represent a preliminary analysis of the current situation.

3   Talking About Talent

"Fourteen-year-old players who would have had to move from the C juniors to the B juniors, were rejected because they were still lacking something physically. At that age, kids are still growing and also one is not simply rejected, but a third B junior team is created for the players if they are technically skilled."
(Johan Cruyff, *Vrij Nederland*, March 1981, quoted in Barend & van Dorp, 2006, p 49)

It is not only in the area of youth soccer that the concept of talent has been the subject of controversial discussions for many years all over the world. The knowledge, abilities and skills that a player acquires during his formation in the junior ranks are considered to be indicative of his future sporting progress. In order to structure a coaching plan for coaches, medical staff, officials and parents, the first general thing to establish is how the concept of talent is defined from different scientific perspectives. Specialist literature usually distinguishes between *static* and *dynamic explanatory approach* (Joch, 1992, p 83). The *static* talent concept comprises four criteria for the definition of a talent:

- Dispositions (ability).

- Willingness (will).

- Social environment (possibilities).

- Results (achievements).

Dynamic talent, on the other hand, is derived from an active and target-oriented process that has two main characteristics:

- The active process of change.

- Guidance through training and competition and pedagogical support.

Joch (1992, p 90) has developed an integrated definition of talent from both explanatory approaches, which is internationally recognized in modern high performance youth sport (Weineck, 2007, p 191).

"A person possesses or is a talent if, based on above-average ability, commitment and the possibilities of their environment (possibly match-proven), he obtains developable performance outcomes that represent the result of an active, pedagogically supported and, internationally guided process of change through training that is purposefully oriented toward a future high (sporting) performance level."

As you will see in the following Chapters, this integrated definition of talent is very similar to the Dutch approach to talent spotting (see Chapters 3.1, 3.2, 4.1, 4.2 and 6.4) and therefore needs no further explanation at this point (see van Barneveld & Vervoorm, 1997, p 9; Pabst, 2001). Instead, the interested reader should refer to:

- The current findings from the talent diagnostics and talent prognoses of the Heidelberg, Cologne and Tübingen research groups around Prof. Dr. Klaus Roth (Heidelberg), Prof. Dr. Daniel Memmert (Cologne German Sports University) and Prof. Dr. O. Höner (Tübingen) for motor performance component tactics in sports games (with emphasis on soccer) (see Memmert & Roth, 2003, pp 44-70).

- the implementation and analysis of computer-supported testing for prognosis-oriented "talent" development in soccer by the Austrian R. Werthner (2001, pp 6-12) (see also Neumann, 2009, pp 129-135).

The latter, which is also used in FC Bayern Munich's talent diagnostics, could, using the talent criterion "trainability" (Hohmann, 2001, p 141), be used as a dynamic talent diagnosis method in high performance youth soccer.

3.1   Talent Spotting

Talent spotting in Dutch soccer represents a special challenge due to the highly complex nature of the performance requirements and the size of the country. If we consider the current international status of diagnostics in high performance youth soccer, despite significantly improved instruments for prognoses regarding conditioning, technique and tactics, there is still a high degree of prognosis inaccuracy, as they concentrate mainly on the future performance of the players concerned. In general, it can be established that "at the start of a high performance sporting training program ... the suitability of an athlete cannot be determined with sufficient accuracy until high performance age has been reached" (Weineck, 2007, p 204). Furthermore, new talent diagnosis procedures are very time consuming and labor intensive. Along with this, there is, as in high performance youth soccer in all countries, the problem of the so-called "theory practice and/or practice theory gap," meaning is it possible when talent spotting to combine sports science findings with subjective empirical knowledge derived from the practice of soccer so that a transfer into soccer practice is actually possible (see van Barnefeld & Vervoorm, 1997, p 10, et al.)?

As you will discover in the following chapters, Dutch associations and clubs are trying, with the participation of sport science, to develop talent spotting models and procedures that involve criteria that can be derived from matches. The following high performance sport basic principle is therefore supported in the Netherlands. "The criteria for suitability

must be derived from the structure of the peak performance level to be aimed for at a later date" (Hofmann & Schneider, 1985, p 49).

3.1.1 Talent Scouting

Precisely because of the complexity of soccer talent spotting and procedure criteria and because the establishment of a soccer-specific catalogue of features is always dependent upon the objective identification of constitutional, social, physical and mental features and/or feature complexes, associations and clubs are developing guidebooks to help during talent scouting and in coaching these players according to their performance level (see KNVB, 1996, p 34). The KNVB has formed stages to avoid the over or under training of talented youngsters in the training and development process that can lead to disgruntlement and a lack of motivation. The efficiency of the established selection process also impacts on the financial and organizational elements and structures of the association, regional associations and clubs.

As well as the talent scouting by the abovementioned institutions in the Netherlands, a "well functioning scouting system is the basis of and determines the quality of all talent development activities" according to Kormelink (1999, p 13). The scouting system should therefore be adapted to the content of each age group and "players from the

B Juniors must possess different qualities than players from the D juniors" (KNVB, 1996, p 34). In the Netherlands, mastery of the match and the training process is the context for the scout's analysis and selection of talent.

According to the KNVB (ibid), ball control (technical abilities and skills) and game intelligence are the key parameters in the selection of talent. The physical coaching of juniors is considered a less significant factor. The KNVB supports the training of talent scouts, who represent, according to the opinion of the KNVB, the cornerstone of the entire youth development program in the Netherlands: "Scouting, the identification of talent, forms the foundation of the whole talent development program (ibid, p 37).

3.1.2   Youth Talent Scouting by the KNVB

In the Netherlands, it is assumed that the selection process in clubs and associations is not clear unless the selection criteria are transparent. The criteria upon which an assessment is based should be evident in matches and, in particular, the individual ability and skills of youth players from D juniors onward should be taken into consideration. Usually, F juniors and E juniors are considered to be too young for scouting purposes because the scouting process itself can often have a negative influence on the players' personality development and hence their playing development at that age. That means in the Netherlands that KNVB scouts, who usually scout from D juniors level upward, do not lead training sessions, "...but let the kids play, and during and after a match establish the criteria. This only involves individual qualities of a talent within the team process" (van Amstel, 28.1.2003). So scouting is more of an observation process that focuses on the following criteria:

> "Ball possession by your team; ball possession of the opposing team and the switch from ball possession to losing the ball and vice versa: In these match moments we can see how the talent behaves in certain situations."
>
> (van Loon et al., 1998, p 34)

The young players are also analyzed from a position-specific point of view, which means they should have specific abilities and skills in offensive and/or defensive game situations that are typical of their playing position. (see Kormelink, 1999, p 15).

3.1.3 Youth Talent Scouting by SC Heerenveen[3]

At SC Heerenveen, scouting generally takes place at junior[4] and senior levels.

At the junior level, there are two different types of scouting:

- Scouting of E and D juniors (for soccer schools)

- Youth scouting of C to A juniors (see van't Haar, 1999a, p 43)

At the core of the work of the SC Heerenveen scouting department is communication with other scouts from the Netherlands and observing the matches of the KNVB national team. Furthermore, scouting also takes place in regions of the former Soviet republics, Germany and Belgium and especially in Scandinavia, which is particularly favored by the SC Heerenveen scouts because "the Scandinavian talents can adapt very quickly to the Dutch way of playing and living" (ibid, p 44). SC Heerenveen also works with scouts who continuously observe the development of young talented players in international leagues. Like the KNVB (see Chapter 3.2), SC Heerenveen is particularly careful not to remove talented young players from their familiar surroundings too soon. "At 13, 14 years old, talented, foreign young players are too young to move to the Netherlands," says the former pro coach at SC Heerenveen and KNVB Association Coach, Foppe de Haan (currently Ajax Capetown) (quoted by Kormelink & Seeverens, 1999b, p 2).

SC Heerenveen looks at five aspects in its scouting:

1. Physical ability

2. Technical ability and skills

3. Resilience

4. Personality structure

5. Do the young talents have something special? (see van't Haar, 1999a, p 45)

When working with C juniors and above, the top scout primarily looks for specific qualities in the player such as concrete defensive play by a central defender, as demonstrated in positional play on the pitch.

---

3   Dutch national league club SC Heerenveen is the leading club in the province of Friesland. The club was founded in 1920, played in the 1993 Cup Final and was runner-up in 2000.

4   The terms *junior* and *youth* are interchangeable.

As position-specific training is not supposed to take place in the E and D juniors in The Netherlands, in these age groups, SC Heerenveen primarily scouts for technical ability and skills.

Young players who are particularly talented can play in the D1 and C2 junior teams of VV Heerenveen, partner club of SC Heerenveen. This intermediate step is necessary because in the Netherlands, the national soccer league is not allowed to organize matches for E and D junior teams.

All other scouted talent in the E and D juniors therefore remain at their home clubs and their associated social environments. SC Heerenveen has also abandoned its so-called *talent days* for these age groups, as is customary at clubs like Ajax Amsterdam and Bayern Munich. The scouted E and D juniors can only train together at the SC Heerenveen soccer school on Wednesdays, as the coaches, pitches and equipment are available there.[5] At the start of the older C junior age group, the outstanding youngsters at SC Heerenveen can play and be directly nurtured by the club (see van't Haar, 1999a, p 46). SC Heerenveen wants these special arrangements to allow them to achieve an uninterrupted scouting, which, in the long term, leads into an uninterrupted, practical talent nurturing. The main purpose of SC Heerenveen's talent scouting is, as well as optimizing its own talent nurturing program, spotting talent for the benefit of its own professional team.

3.1.4   Youth Talent Scouting by NEC Nijmegen

On Feb. 19, 2010, Iddo Roscher, U14 coach and "Technical Manager" of the national league club's NEC Soccer Academy (*Voetbalacademie*) was interviewed about talent scouting at NEC Nijmegen, from which the authors have extracted the following quote:

"We don't look so much at whether a youngster plays well or badly. We are more interested in his ability and imagine whether in the **future** he could play well for us, i.e., whether he is capable of improvement. We think a lot about the future and don't always look first at the present. If a player is very developed athletically and wins many tackles for this reason, this doesn't necessarily mean that he is also more talented. He may win the match for the team now, but that does not interest us. We are mainly interested in talent that will find expression in the **future**.

We also consider how we can help and coach the player to make him even better. We also look for things that are harder to teach. The older the player, the harder it is for him to learn or develop new things.

---

5   This regulation is unusual in an international context. Austria Wien and FC Liverpool junior sections start coaching from under 8 or under 9 (see Kubierske & Pabst, 2002, p 35, et al.).

For older players, the first thing we look at is position. For our goals, we interpret certain abilities and skills that a player needs for **position-specific** play. Then we look at the position players themselves. A central defender is assessed differently than a winger.

The abilities and skills that a player must possess are all important, but we mainly focus on the following criteria:

*   **Psychology:** behavior, perseverance, how much "grit" does the player have?

*   **Game intelligence:** during own and opponents' ball possession, feel for game situations, choice of position and ball handling/action on the ball.

*   **Athleticism:** speed, agility.

*   **Tackling.**

*   **Technique**.

Three other criteria are also very important:

- The will to win.

- A willingness to work hard.

- The necessary **parental** support.

Naturally, these criteria are hard to identify. At best, the first two criteria can be observed in the context of a trial. However, I believe that we can improve significantly in these areas.

We look at all F1 and E1 teams within a **25-mile radius** and scout outstanding players, who we then invite to a trial at the group where we analyze how much **talent** this player possesses. If he does well, he also plays in matches.

The region of Cleves (in Germany) falls within this radius, and we also scout here for talent so that we could also accept German players into our coaching program. Current Dutch champions, Twente Enschede, coach many more German players than we do though."

3.2 Talent Development from the Perspective of the KNVB

"There will always be talented players. They occur naturally and are not the result of hard training!"

(Rinus Michels quoted in Verheijen, 1999/2000, p 231)

In order to be able to optimally structure a soccer-specific talent development program, the KNVB talent developers are required to put the characteristic qualities of Dutch soccer into practice.

According to the guidelines of the coaching authority of Dutch soccer, the KNVB Academy in Zeist, there are three key elements for the development of every Dutch soccer talent:

- The player's initiative in all areas.

- The player's dominant position.

- Great attention to the soccer-technical team-building process (KNVB, 1996, p 1).

According to the KNVB, there are different phases to every talent development that should be considered in coaching. In the first phase, *familiarization* with soccer, the player should play with a great deal of enthusiasm and learn how to identify his own possibilities in dealing with and/or in confrontation with himself and his sporting environment. This first phase is characterized as a unit that is achieved through talent (ability), motivation (will) and discipline (hard work)" (Kormelink & Seeverens, 1999d, p 5). The second phase, which emphasizes technical tactical training, is not only concerned with "playing as efficiently, intelligently and creatively as possible" (de Vries & Rossum, 1998, p 23), but also learning to handle mental challenges (see Kormelink & Seeverens, 1999d, p 5). For this reason, for example, Dutch first division club Vitesse Arnhem offers personality training, where players can boost their self-confidence and teamwork in a group (see Vitesse Arnhem, 2002, p 3).

> **Note:** *Bundesliga* team TSV Bayer 04 Leverkusen's youth section adopts the same approach as Vitesse. It operates with a personality training program that emphasizes responsibility, ambition/motivation and identification with the club (see Bayer 04 Leverkusen, 2000, p 16).

In the third phase, the talent should form his "own personality." According to Kormelink and Seeverens (1999d, p 6), this phase involves "the further development of a high-performance sport-oriented personality." In the Netherlands, it is assumed that in team sports like soccer, handball or basketball, players learn a lot from each other. This recognition leads performance-oriented clubs in the Netherlands to form teams of similar performance levels for training and match practice in order to avoid under or over loading talented youngsters. As a result, in Dutch soccer, the task of the youth coach is especially important (see Chapter 5.1). This key role is based, according to Kormelink and Seeverens (1999d, p 6), on the free choice of field activity (age and ability) and the "inspiring and enthusiastic charisma" (ibid) of the coach in the Dutch talent development system.

According to Wien (2001, p 77), who has explored the Spanish and Dutch mentoring concepts in great detail in his numerous publications, a coach of children and youngsters does not need a perfect technical knowledge of soccer, but he must be able to understand and, most importantly, pedagogically develop the child. "The coach focuses not only on technical aspects but also on tactical, physical and mental aspects. It takes time to achieve good performance levels" (ibid).

The role of parents and the family is given special importance in Dutch talent development. Social and familial influences are determining factors in the personality and performance development of talented players. The "pedagogical mentoring" referred to by Kormelink and Seeverens (1999d, p 7) assumes that in the complex training process of talent development the function, "the control of emotions, but this help must always take place in the background." The role of the parents within the triangular "talent, coach, family" relationship should, according to the Dutch model, be structured so that parents and coach are not in competition with each other." (see ibid).

3.3 Talent Development in the Netherlands and Germany as Seen by the Dutch Technical Review, *TrainersMagazine*

Talent development and training go hand in hand for coaches (see Chapters 3 and 5). Why? Because the greater a coach's knowledge and ability, the lower the risk there is of mistakes being made in talent scouting and development. Any bad decisions can be very damaging for countries, associations and clubs in modern professional soccer at the top international level (who are critically dependent on high financial revenues for the securing and optimization of the coaching system).

Comparisons are certainly a tried and tested way of assessing and evaluating the coaching models used from qualitative and quantitative perspectives. However, they are not currently available. Instead, the relevant literature contains subjective judgments that are worthy of future empirical further investigation. Below are two current examples:

*   "We have perhaps the most important coach training system in the world ... We ourselves don't even realize it" (Jan van Dijk [Head Coach of the Dutch national league club VVV Venlo], quoted in Job [2010], p 116).

*   In such a small country, strengths can be grouped differently than in ours. ... The contents are largely the same throughout Europe. The difference is in the way they are taught" (Frank Wormuth [Head of Soccer Coaching Education at the DFB] quoted in Job [2010], p 116).

Both quotes make it clear that it makes basic sense to understand what the other associations and clubs do differently and/or the same in terms of the teaching and practice of contents and methodology in coaching, training and competition. How and whether these differences are integrated into the training structures is a question the authors do not have the space to explore in this book.

Since, at this point, the assessment of Dutch talent development could be important for the topic of our book, *Dutch Soccer Secrets*, the authors asked the editor in chief of the internationally renowned Dutch coaching technical magazine *TrainersMagazine*, Paul van Veen (*www.trainerssite.nl*), about the current state of the development of youth soccer in

the Netherlands and Germany as of Dec. 14, 2009, in Zeist. The authors consider van Veen to be a kind of "wanderer between worlds" of the training and match pitch and writing about soccer training; in other words, the prototype of an internationally experienced soccer expert.

Authors: *Paul, what is special about Dutch talent development?*

PvV: I think that many Dutch coaches train players to play in the first senior team. Winning therefore plays a subordinate role. It sounds simple, but many coaches orient the training content in this way.

Many coaches focus on creative playmaking as a way of improving soccer playing. Even if this does not always work, the players should always try it again! Many coaches also think totally offensively and place the emphasis on opening up the game!

31

Authors: *What is special about the children's developmental stage?*

PvV: It is hard to say what is special. We must be careful with which culture we make this comparison. What is special in the Netherlands is that most amateur clubs are much more than just soccer clubs. They organize a lot of other, non-sporting activities. So the club is more than just a place where people learn to play soccer.

Most kids are trained by volunteers (especially fathers). The way of working is different club to club. The philosophy is either determined by the club or by individual coaches. For the last few years, people have been using circuit training, when, for instance, from 5pm to 6pm, four or more teams can train on one pitch at the same time. Four different training games are played that are changed after 15 minutes! It is a very simple, but structured, way to learn to play soccer!

In the Netherlands, the F and E juniors play 7v7 on half a pitch. The D juniors play on a whole pitch.

At the moment, the Coerver Method is all the rage in the Netherlands, as is the KNVB vision. The use of resistance in all training drills is commonplace. However, in the last 10 years, more and more coaches have been choosing 1v0 situation training, mostly alone with a ball, possibly with cone markers or passive opponents. This focus was rather oriented toward the Coerver Method than the KNVB vision. Different coaches who work with the visie (vision) are contracted to foreign clubs (e.g., Ricardo Moniz at RB Salzburg, Pepijn Lijnders at FC Porto or René Meulensteen at Manchester United).

Authors: *What is special about the Dutch youth level?*

PvV: Many teams get their "permanent" coach in the juniors. For C1, B1 and A1, they have their own coach; for bigger clubs also for C2, B2 and A2. It is usually mandatory to have a coaching license!

Authors: *What is absolutely critical to look for in the transition from juniors to seniors?*

PvV: What strikes me is that many players stay in their clubs from juniors onward. Of course, a few players try to reach the highest level. But most players remain loyal to their clubs. It is often the case that the smallest clubs attract the most loyalty.

Authors: *You talk to many Dutch youth coaches, what do you think is positive or negative in Dutch youth soccer culture?*

PvV: I notice that many coaches remain totally fanatically loyal to their vision and desire to coach. You get the feeling that winning is not the most important thing. It is all about coaching the players and playing soccer for fun. However, one negative aspect is, for example, that coaches allow too many "long balls" to be played. If you want to win, then please make it look nice!

Authors: *You are an amateur coach, too! What is your opinion of the Dutch amateur clubs?*

PvV: As I said before, the soccer club is more than a soccer club!

Authors: *What is a typical Dutch youth coach like?*

PvV: A good Dutch youth coach teaches the players how they can play soccer autonomously. We consider it to be important that players take the initiative for themselves during the game. A good youth coach also asks questions instead of just giving orders. The players must find their own solutions during matches. In other cultures, players often look to the coach when they can't find solutions. We don't want that in the Netherlands! Players must find their own solutions by themselves!

Authors: *What is currently more important in youth soccer, technique, mentality, or something else?*

PvV: For a few years, technique has been ubiquitous. This also copies a development toward commercial soccer schools, where the players do extra work on their technique alongside their club training. This works very successfully in many regions. The area of mental coaching is also growing in popularity. However, as before, the focus is clearly on technique, and everything else is secondary!

Authors: *What do you think is good about German youth soccer?*

PvV: I have a certain image of German youth soccer. When I watch German youth teams playing soccer, it strikes me that they play a bit like the Dutch: a lot of combination play, good positional play and good individuality with a lot of creativity.

In Germany, I think a huge development has taken place. If you combine this modern way of playing soccer with your enormous German willpower, then you will be very good in the future!

4   The KNVB Philosophy

> "Everything that goes into too much detail is often so boring. But for those who need to know the details, it is a necessary evil, for nothing exists for its own sake."
> (Johan Cruyff, March 1985; quoted in Barend & van Dorp, 2006, p 59)

The Dutch soccer youth development program is implemented in a country of around 16 million inhabitants. The KNVB is, as the professional organization and therefore as the supervisory body, responsible for the content and structure of the organization and development of youth soccer. In the past few decades, it has evolved from a national sports association with exclusive responsibility in the area of league and coaches' training to an association that also formulates and implements visions. The KNVB has a great reputation and is admired worldwide for its consistent, transparent and very effective youth development philosophy. The "total vision of youth soccer" (KNVB, 2001, p 1), which was presented to the public by the KNVB in 2001 as the "Masterplan of Youth Soccer" (ibid), describes the path of Dutch talent development. This master plan is still valid and is assessed below by the current head coach at the KNVB, Nico Romeijn, in an interview with the authors on Feb. 4, 2010:

> "However, it is totally serious and of vital importance to have a plan of how we envisage and therefore deal with talent development. The focus is on the players, who must have the best coaching, whatever their level. But this is only possible with a plan and with good coaches who don't just want to coach for coaching's sake but want to use their coaching methods to develop the players."

4.1   The Dutch Youth Soccer Master Plan

The master plan gives information about the basic key points in the development of high performance and less serious Dutch youth soccer players. In the KNVB, currently around half a million youth soccer players are actively involved in training and playing. The openness of this coaching process makes it possible in particular for the less "serious" young players to switch to the high performance training branch if they show enough talent and willpower.

The master plan documents in two steps how the high performance youth player and the youth casual player can be coached in soccer. In *basic coaching*, all youth players are familiarized with activities that are focused on pedagogical guidance. These activities also include highly qualified coaching. This first step in the coaching of youth players in the Netherlands is oriented toward physical improvement of the players based on education and learning. Both steps, pedagogical guidance and highly qualified coaching, are inseparably linked in the Netherlands and can be represented as follows:

- Maintenance and structure of children's teams.

- The reduction of downtime in the youth area.

- Special training courses for youth coaches working with young children.

- More attention on indoor soccer in the youth area.

- More attention for talented youngsters in handicapped soccer.

- Soccer activities for kids from socially and economically deprived backgrounds.

- The development of a concept of pedagogical mentoring in the youth area

- The appointment of children's regional coaches by the association (see KNVB, 2001, p 2).

The master plan also includes such activities as the KNVB initiative "Grenzloos Voetbal" (soccer without limits) (Stoop, 1999, p 57), in which young people from social and financially disadvantaged backgrounds can participate in the Dutch sporting culture.

The master plan therefore offers club coaches general guidelines that are intended to contribute to the expansion of the methodological repertoire. In particular, the idea of the renaissance "of street soccer must be included in the training process" (Kormelink & Seeverens, 1999c, p 13). At this point, it should be emphasized that high performance youth soccer can (and should) always incorporate the playful and creative character of the game. The KNVB also focuses on the coaching of "top talents" (KNVB, 2001, p 9):

> "In high performance talent development, we must single out individual talents so that later the best talents can play in a team and ultimately achieve positive results in senior soccer!"
>
> (van Amstel, 28.1.2003)

This brings us to the second step in the master plan: every talent should get the chance to become a top player (see KNVB, 2001, p 9). To ensure this goal can be attained in the future through high quality coaching and guidance, the KNVB appoints working groups that ensure the development of the demand-specific content and methods of the master plan (see Hubers, 2000, p 49). Below are examples of the basic innovations that the master plan has put into practice on the second step of the high performance youth development program:

- Setting up new junior international teams: under 21 for men and under 23 for women.

- Reforming the Dutch youth plan.

- Optimizing the performance of the youth leagues.

- Replacement of the second team of professional clubs by an under-23 team.

- A new coaching structure for youth soccer coaches.

- Licensing requirement for all professional soccer clubs.

- A grading system for all professional club youth sections.

- Appointment of regional coaches in the association (see KNVB, 2001, p 2).

The master plan in the Netherlands always stands for the *totalvision* (total vision) of soccer. This means that the KNVB attempts to represent all the tasks and goals of Dutch youth soccer in a compact form. In this ongoing developmental process, no detail should be overlooked (ibid). This *vision* of Dutch youth soccer involves all clubs participating in the development of the sport with the aid of the KNVB.

4.2   Soccer as a Learning Process

The Dutch philosophy of soccer puts the emphasis on action, as learning should mainly be done through practice (see van Lingen, 2001, p. 9). Therefore, there is no "practice theory and theory practice gap" in the Netherlands (see Smink, 2003, p. 21). The importance of theoretical knowledge is instead considered a (theoretical) building block that can be used to analyze training management and coaching within a team or for individual talent development (see Kormelink, 1999, p 11).

The above-mentioned idea of street soccer that the German sports researcher K. Roth terms a "model of incidental incubation" (2000), should in another step be supplemented by sports-specific coaching in clubs and associations (see Michels & Vergoossen, 2001). The training sessions therefore include different game and match forms that not only enable the juniors to implicitly learn how to play soccer through game situations in the match itself, but the coaches in the Netherlands can explicitly grasp the intrinsic possibilities of the game in order to derive and communicate help and tasks for the juniors' learning process.

The game in the Netherlands therefore constitutes the primary key factor for managing the learning process of the young players, which the coach provides for the young players in a compact form: "the game is the test" (van Lingen, 2001, p 12). Dutch junior players thus experience the learning process as a "soccer learning process" in which the game is the focal point of all considerations (see KNVB, 2001, p. 2).

4.2.1 "Techniek, Inzicht, Communicatie" – the TIC Model

The elements that characterize match play are included by the KNVB in the TIC Model. In the Netherlands, this model upholds the motto "if you want to play soccer, you must have TIC" (van Lingen, 2001, p 3), the contents of which are described below.

Techniek (technique):
The KNVB sees this as the presence of technical abilities and skills that enable a player of any age to play soccer.

Inzicht (game intelligence/insight):
(Game) intelligence is understood here as a kind of "demeanor" in the player that classifies and evaluates match actions in a situation-appropriate way. It is mainly based on perception processes and "prior knowledge" in the form of commonly occurring basic patterns (see Michels, 2000a, p 193).

Communicatie (Communication):
The TIC Model attaches great importance to the attention players give individual and team-oriented play.[6] It is expressed in match play and training by means of non-verbal and verbal communication:

- Coaching between players.

- Coaching between coach and players (and vice versa).

- Instructions by the referee and linesmen.

Communication is also accompanied by internal and external perception stimuli:

- Constantly changing match game situations.

---

6   Game actions address personal and environmental aspects. They represent prototypes of the assertion of will. See the works of van Lingen (2001, p 3) and van Lingen & Pauw (2001a, p 6) for further information.

- Pitch and weather conditions.

- Type and weight of ball.

- Color of jerseys.

- Number of spectators and stadium/ground size.

- The importance of the match.

- Press, radio and TV.

- Verbal and non-verbal communication of the spectators, etc.

For the KNVB, the communication building block is the leading component of the coaching program in the Netherlands because it initiates the optimal development of the player as he learns crucial information for the game of soccer.

The KNVB considers the three building blocks of the TIC model as mutually influential; they cannot stand alone and still be effective. "All three components influence each other. The greater the TIC, the more pronounced the playing ability" (van Lingen & Pauw, 2001a, p. 6).

In the Netherlands, other models exist at club level that mainly consider the qualifications and coaching in the area of technical abilities and skills (technique) as the leading component in the coaching of Dutch youth.

Using the clubs Ajax Amsterdam, Twente Enschede, NEC Nijmegen, the soccer academies of Rotterdam, and the enterprise of sportpartners, Chapters 5, 6, 7, 9 and 10 show that philosophies and concepts in the Netherlands are developed and implemented so they reflexively accompany the master plan: "Many roads lead to Rome" (Fons van der Brande, [Head of the firm *sportpartners*] in an interview conducted Feb. 10, 2010 [Chapter 7.4]).

4.3   Age Groups in Talent Coaching

The discussion about the division of talent coaching into age groups and/or also training years is a very controversial one around the world and is therefore dealt with differently in coaching practice (see Ruiz, 2002, p. i-xi; Lames et al, 2008, pps 4-9, Hyballa & te Poel, 2009, pps 99-111). The KNVB divides talent development into the children and junior, both of which have specific age ranges.

4.3.1   Children (Pupils)

The KNVB children's section spans four age categories: the mini-school kids and the F, E and D juniors.

For the mini-school kids, the KNVB organizes 4v4 games on a small pitch.

The KNVB sets out the following development-specific parameters for soccer playing and training for the developmental phase of F juniors (ages 5-8):

- The children's concentration is limited, so detailed explanations by the coach do not yet lead to effective development (see van Langen, 2001, p 5).

- The child usually does not yet want to play soccer in a team because

- "the child is individually inclined" (Verheijen, 1997, p. 228). For this reason, playing with the ball is the focus of this coaching phase.

- The F juniors are very eager to learn and learn very quickly. The experience of success provides lasting encouragement for the development of children of this age (see Stoop, 2001, p. 39).

The KNVB summarizes these parameters as follows:

"For the F juniors, individual ball possession and 'running after the ball' are key. Avoid long explanations, let them experience, let them watch and copy" (KNVB Academy, 2010a, translated from the Dutch).

The E juniors (ages 8-10) are characterized by the KNVB by the following features:

- Realizing for the first time that soccer is a team sport in which everyone can play a part.

- The exclusive "ego orientation" of children diminishes, and they learn to distinguish between "who can play well or less well" and develop an independent and self-confident way of playing (Bode, 2001, p 26).

- F and E juniors play 7v7 on half a large pitch.

The KNVB characterizes this coaching phase broadly as "E juniors must have the chance to practice many abilities and discover solutions in match situations. An E junior is target-oriented and wants much more to work with the others than an F junior" (KNVB Academy, 2010a, translated from the Dutch).

For the D juniors (ages 10-12), the KNVB considers the following features to be particularly characteristic:

- The D juniors are in the "prepubescent phase" in which body size and musculature are in a well-balanced relationship to each other, which means their coordination skills are considerable.

- This phase of development is particularly suited to the initiation of "game intelligence" (van Lingen, 2001, p 6), or the initiation of ability (or abilities) and varying ability (or abilities) in convergent thought and game creativity, which means they have spontaneous ideas in the form of rare, but game-relevant, patterns (divergent thinking) (see Sternberg & Lubart, 1995).

- In this phase, the D juniors understand the rules of the game and the most important features of defensive and offensive play. On this fertile soil, the foundations for an 11- a side match and the transition into the junior ranks of the KNVB talent development can thrive. The pitch size and number of players is now viewed more critically. "From D juniors onward, players play 11v11 on the full-sized pitch. We see this rather critically in the D juniors, and perhaps there are also changes to be made there. The only thing that is currently different in the D juniors is the goal kick from the 16m line and the corner kick from halfway along the endline" (Romeijn from 2.4.2010).

What the players learn may be summarized as follows: "D juniors play 11-a side matches and are keen to learn in training how they can deploy their abilities in a 'big game' of soccer. The coach orientates his training so that he can teach this experience through simplified soccer forms" (KNVB Academy, 2010a, translated from the Dutch).

4.3.2   Junior Level

From the point of view of the Dutch Soccer Association, in the C juniors (ages 12-14), the following parameters should be taken into consideration for the planning, implementation and evaluation of the entire training process:

*   Training of perceptive abilities focusing on soccer action speed. This should be accompanied by an enhancement of playing enjoyment and the players' performance levels.

*   The start of puberty with only limited resilience "from agile, well-proportioned and smooth players who have never had to struggle with injuries, they turn, - sometimes overnight, into tall, gangly beanpoles with wooden movements who are constantly grappling with some injury or other" (Kormelink & Seeverens, 1999b, p 48).

*   In the C junior teams, it is possible to identify introverted and extroverted players who are still unable to control their bodies independently (keyword Character Building: see ibid p 53).

The KNVB's talent development in the B junior age group (ages 14-16) primarily takes into account:

*   The sometimes significant physical changes (increase in strength, balancing out of physical proportions, increase in coordination, etc.).

*   The frequently accompanying emotional upheaval and declining motivation (see ibid, p 65)

As in the B juniors, playing speed increases due to the average increased performance level, which particularly leads to clearly increased time, accuracy and complex pressure during the match. The different pressure factors must therefore be compatible with the above-mentioned physical and psycho-social performance factors.

The A juniors (ages 16-18) are usually characterized by a marked physical development. Their physical proportions, with appropriate training, gain in symmetry and the increase in strength has a thoroughly positive effect on acceleration and speed. As for mental changes, in training it can be established that realistic self-assessment, striving for autonomy and acknowledgement as an equal partner, and critical and reflex ability increase.

These positive mental and physical changes lay the foundations for self-confident behavior on and off the pitch and for the accurate, variable and quick transfer of basic tasks in the relevant position on the team.

In all age groups, the Dutch always place the ball at the focus of talent development (see Hyballa, 2001a, p 40).

4.4   The KNVB Match System

The current match program in KNVB youth soccer is divided into six performance categories (see KNVB, 2010).

1. National A juniors *eredivisie* (national league)

2. Two national first divisions (regional *eerste divisies*)

3. Two divisions, according to district

4. The third divisions

5. *Hoofdklasse* (amateur classes)

6. The first, second and third classes

4.5   The "Five-Phase Model" of Dutch Talent Development

Based on the seven different age groups mentioned above, the KNVB has developed the "Five-Phase Model" of Dutch talent development. This model is based on the idea that "even this phased model is just a rough guideline of a possible talent development system that can work, but if a goal is reached in one phase, the player can also cope with the next phase without too much trouble" (van Amstel, 28.01.2003). What does that mean exactly?

In the **first phase**, "the ball is the goal!" This phase is also termed the starting phase (see van Lingen, 2001, p 28). In this phase, the children should experience the acquisition of technical abilities. "The aim is to control the ball" (van Lingen & Pauw, 2001a, p 23). In order to develop ball control, the children play on small pitches to allow for greater ball contact. The KNVB also calls "free play," or *mikken* (Stoop, 2001, p 40), in which the F juniors experience their own "urge to move" and can discover their playful imagination in free soccer play. "Just let the kids play for fun" in order to guide, but not control, them into the next phase (Mariman, 2002a, p 20).

The **second phase** is characterized by the "basic functional playing maturity" (van Lingen, 2001, p 28) of the 7- to 12-year-old kids. "The ball is the focus" (van Lingen & Pauw, 2001a, p 22). This playing maturity in Dutch soccer should be learned in basic form through simple and constantly repeated play situations, which help the kids to improve their technical abilities and skills. The basic forms are characterized by their "soccer-specific nature, by many repetitions, by adaptation to the age-appropriate soccer level and by the many possibilities of adequate, situation-appropriate coaching" (van Lingen, 2001, p 28). In this phase, according to the TIC model, the kids should learn the basics of game intelligence. Therefore, the method in this phase of game development is closely linked to the demand of the game. The KNVB assumes that in this stage, the development of all techniques can be learned through playing.

In the **third phase**, the focus should not only be on the ball. The coaching of individual technical abilities and skills is considered here. In this training phase for 12 to 16-year-olds, "the focus is on the game" (van Lingen, 2001, p 28.) This primarily involves an intensive learning and training process, which enhances "the development of tactical understanding through the recognizing of game plans and through general starting points in the key moments when the opposing team and their team are in possession of the ball" Kormelink & Seeverens, 1999b, p 67). Thus, (game) intelligence becomes increasingly valued and is combined with position-specific coaching. The coaching of the basic functional playing maturity should be replaced by group and team tactical goals, whereby the technical development of the juniors is integrated with the tactical and communicative elements of the TIC model. Communication between team and coach and within the team itself is practiced actively in this developmental phase so that play situations on the pitch can be increasingly analyzed and resolved from individual, group and team tactical points of view and also developed through the juniors' responsive actions (see Hyballa, 2001d, p. 42).

In the **fourth phase**, the 16- to 18-year-olds are told that: "the game is the goal" (van Lingen, 2001, p. 28). Results and league rankings become increasingly important in this phase: "They must learn to win instead of losing" (Michels, 2000a, p 164). Team success is the priority and positional play tasks should be optimized in this developmental phase. The juniors should be trained to become "specialists" (van Lingen, 2001, p 28) and to prove themselves in their playing position from an individual-tactical point of view. In the training process, the coaching focus is on position play. Alongside this focus, mutual match coaching forms the second "pillar" of game-intrinsic procedural coaching in this developmental phase (see Hyballa, 2001d, p 42). In this phase, alternative solutions should be analyzed, communicated and transferred into concrete action instructions/keywords for the match (coaching).

The **fifth phase** is characterized by the concept that "mastery is the goal" for players over the age of 18 (van Lingen, 2001, p 28). In the fifth phase, the junior should reach his individual personal playing potential, or optimal playing maturity. In this last phase of the KNVB coaching curriculum, the players are familiarized with the specific technical demands in concrete playing positions in individual training. The further development of the team-tactical process completes this training phase (see Michels, 2000a, p 167). The KNVB does not end this phase with a fixed age limit (see van Lingen, 2001, p 28), for the young senior players should learn "real match play qualities, the correct attitude toward training and professional lifestyle" (Michels, 2000a, p 167-168) en route to becoming professional players. The phase model of the KNVB usually ends when the player becomes a senior.

5

5 The Dutch Youth Coach in Clubs and Associations

"Our advantage is that we are a very small country. Every day, the best can play and train here. Soccer is the number one sport. Every small village has its club. The first thing we do when eleven people come together is play soccer."
(Remy Reynierse, coach's trainer at the KNVN Academy in Zeist, quoted in Bertram, May 2010, p 117)

In the Dutch coaching philosophy, there is a clear separation between seniors and juniors/children (see Kormelink & Seeverens, 1998b, p 69).

Iddo Roscher, technical manager of the NEC Nijmegen Soccer Academy, noted three *qualification features of a youth coach* in the Netherlands back in 2000 in an interview (ibid, Feb. 10, 2000).

First feature: the development of talent is the focus of his daily work.

Second feature: the youth coach is not defined by the match results of his junior teams. He remains firmly in the background in public.

Third feature: the youth coach knows the different phases and goals of talent development and masters the didactic and methodical transfer of them into practice.

5.1 The Tasks of the Youth Coach

Peter van Amstel (Jan. 28, 2003), Association coach in the KNVB district east, sees the tasks (and role) of a youth coach in Dutch soccer very differently. He emphasizes "that a good children's coach who works at the grassroots level is completely different from a good youth coach who trains an A junior team and vice versa." From this, it can be deduced that in the Netherlands, ideally every age group has a coach who can meet the specific needs of that age group:

• In the first phase of talent development, the coach should have positive charisma and also work enthusiastically. He should set a playful tone in everyday training and always give the children positive feedback (see Kormelink & Seeverens, 1999d, p 7).

47

- In the juniors, the youth coach should work both as a teacher and also increasingly as an expert with technical expertise and experience.

The state of development of the children and juniors therefore determines the work of the youth coach in the Netherlands and requires of him a special ability to adapt to the most diverse expectations (player, club/association, parents and media) in his role as youth coach.

Dutch youth coaches are also expected to think long-term and not to work from match day to match day (see van Lingen, 2001, p 5). "The good, responsible youth coach places himself firmly in the background" (Hub Stevens, former head youth coordination of PSV Eindhoven and current head coach at Red Bull Salzburg; quoted after Brüggemann, 2000, p 60).

What a typical daily routine for a Dutch youth coach of a national league club actually looks like can be seen in the following extract from the personal interview with René Hake, Junior Head Coach and U23 coach at the 2010 Dutch champions Twente Enschede (ibid, 1.12.2010 in Enschede; see also Chapter 6.5):

> "Every morning we get to the club around 8:30 am. At 8:30 am, the coaching staff of the first senior team and the U23 exchange comments about players and carry out the corresponding planning. We prepare for the U23 individual training sessions and individual and group talks. Then, from 10 am to noon, training takes place. Lunch is from 12:30 pm to 1 pm. After lunch, the coaching staff thinks about the ensuing planning. Once again we prepare training in smaller groups, followed by training from 2:30 pm to 4:30 pm. After training, there are individual chats until 6 pm. Depending on the program, individual players are still scouted."

From this account, it is evident that the work of a head youth coach at a professional Dutch club comprises organization, training planning and monitoring, training implementation, match supervision, following up of training and matches, swapping between the spheres of activities, player scouting and further training and may be considered a thoroughly comprehensive, complex and responsible activity.

As already mentioned in Chapter 3.3, talent development in the Netherlands is always considered from the point of view of "taking the long view and perspective" (see Hof, 2001, p 52). The youth coach is also considered to have the role and function of "-developer" with a great aptitude for the promotion of creativity. This does not mean that no importance is attached to positive match results in the juniors. Danny Blind, 2003 youth coordinator of the Dutch champions Ajax Amsterdam, emphasizes in a personal interview the positive effects of successful match results in the juniors on the reputation of the youth coach and the standing of the club in the Netherlands (ibid, May 8, 2003 in Amsterdam). In modern youth soccer, this aspect is enhanced by the perspective of experience and orientation. The importance of targeted group-specific communication therefore increasingly shifts into the expanded focus of the training of youth coaches in the Netherlands and should always be compared with the exclusive sporting demands on a youth coach.

5.1.1   The Tasks of the Youth Coach
at Dutch National League Club NEC Nijmegen

Most junior teams in Dutch national league clubs play in the highest junior playing classes (see Chapter 4.4). This means that the youth coach at Dutch national league club NEC Nijmegen is responsible for combining match and result-oriented training and development orientation toward high-performance youth soccer. The club not only values the leading of training sessions and the coaching of matches, but it also limits how many players from its own junior ranks take the "leap into the first team" (see Hyballa, 1999, p 4). The youth coach also undertakes talent scouting duties. All players who play at NEC Nijmegen are "...scouted players, who were discovered at other clubs in and around Nijmegen" (ibid, p 5). The NEC area for talent scouting includes the Dutch-German border area. Van Lingen (2001, p14) terms the additional work of the youth coach "active scouting." German junior players are particularly important for Dutch clubs as they bring "typical German qualities," such as tackling strength, athleticism and discipline (see Boesten, no year). René Hake, head junior coach and U23 coach for reigning Dutch champion Twente Enschede, underlines this aspect in the following excerpt from a personal interview on Jan. 12, 2010 in Enschede (see also Chapter 6.5).

"Here, we coach 160 players from U12 to U23, 29 of whom are German, who play in eight different teams. That is 20%. There are big differences between German and Dutch players, which can be expressed roughly as follows: Germans have much better soccer discipline than Dutch players. In matches against German teams, it strikes me that they are much more geared to counterattacking. They often stand together in a block in which even the strikers play defensively. This makes the spaces compact and narrow. They can play like this for 90 minutes; it is fantastic. When they have won possession of the ball, they quickly play deep and try to play to the strikers who are often good at finding space. When they have possession of the ball, they often try to play forward from behind. The discipline of the Germans is unique and often leads to interesting matches. That is why we try to make sure that all teams play friendly matches against German sides up to eight times a year!"

It is also important to those in charge of NEC Nijmegen "that the coach chooses the right type of drills and training games and critically assesses and constantly corrects the players." Also, "the active promotion" of individual players on and off the training and match pitch is ensured by the youth coaches (Roscher, Feb. 10, 2000). As already explained in Chapter 5.1, educating talents to be independent and to emphasize constant communication and interaction between the juniors and the youth coaches (and vice versa) represent key contents of the NEC Nijmegen philosophy:

1. Preparation and transition into the professional ranks

2. "Holding their own in pro soccer"

3. "The development of playing personalities" (see Hyballa, 1999, p 9)

5.1.2 The Tasks of the Youth Coach in KNVB East District[7]

The tasks of the youth coach (association coach) in the association are characterized by the following foci:

First focus: the scouting of talented players from the clubs.

Second focus: the promotion of the development of the talent in the playing process.

Third focus: the supervision of the coach training process (see Kormelink, 2001a, p 32).

The work of the association coach centers on the scouting of talent from the different regions.

The KNVB comprises six regional associations (districts).[8] The main task of the association coach is the filling of the association squads in the different age groups. "For this reason, he watches and selects the championship matches of the junior teams, but he constantly communicates with the team coach" (van Amstel, 1.28.2003). The priority is the individual talent and their coaching. The association coach is supported by his regional coach (*regiocoach*). The KNVB district East is further sub-divided into 10 regions so that the association coach receives from the regional coaches content statements about the talents in the regions. The area of responsibility in the different regions requires organizational skill on the part of the coaches and regular interaction with the club coaches. The tasks of the youth coach in the association (district) and region (regio) are "more passive, as we don't lead training sessions, but just spot talented players and encourage them with comparison matches with other talents in the association" (ibid). The association coach and regional coach are therefore "coaches for the clubs" and "observers of players" (ibid).

---

7   The district Oost is one of the six regional associations of the KNVB with headquarters in Deventer.
8   The six regional associations of the KNVB are the *districte noord*, based in Heerenveen, *oost* based in Deventer, *west* 1 in Amsterdam, *west* 2 in Rotterdam, *zuid* 1 in Breda and *zuid* 2 in Nieuwstadt.

5.2 From Coaching and Teambuilding to Management Style in Dutch Youth Coaching

The term *coaching*[9] is generally used to mean "all the advice and guidance from the coach that lead to an improvement in performance in training and competition (Röthig, 1992, p 102). With regard to soccer, "coaching is the soccer-specific guidance of the player in competition, based on the data and impressions gained in training" (Rutemöller, 2001, p 6). In the Netherlands, coaching is geared to each respective age group. Child players should be positively supported in their playing development with verbal encouragement. To this end, van Amstel (1.28.2010) includes "ausrasen," the concept that the kids should motivate themselves for matches and be mentored by the youth coach through a brief, verbal presentation of the basic ideas of the game. The junior-level coach provides the young players with more precise verbal support and can, according to van Lingen (2001, p 13-14), even enter into a critical dialogueue with them. Kormelink and Seeverens (2001, p 4) suggest that the youth coach should analyze the last match and, through individual talks with each player, prepare them for their specific tasks. This procedure has proven very effective in the individual development of talent. During the match, the coaching emphasis should be on game observation and giving short, clear and comprehensible instructions to the players, such as "take the ball to the goal" (van Lingen, 2001, p 21). In Dutch youth soccer, the only details that should be discussed briefly are those with a (positive) stimulating contribution for the players. Coaching in the youth training process is thus primarily based on match analysis and long-term coaching emphases (see Kormelink & Seeverens, 2000, p 57). Coaching before, during and after the match is an important aid for the coach in identifying whether the team and/or individual players are receptive to the coach's advice.

For the KNVB, it is fundamental that the youth coach can identify and learn the complex demand profile of coaching in Dutch youth soccer. The learning process is divided into five sections:

---

9   In this book, the term *coaching* means the *mentoring, encouraging* and *advising* of talented young players. In sports science, it is considered from different perspectives (see Seeger, 2008, ps 5-8). The terms *coach* and *trainer* are used interchangeably in this source and stand for the youth coach who coaches his team.

First Section: Knowledge and intelligence in soccer

The coach should know himself and how he reacts in certain situations. Only when he has acquired and reflected upon these experiences can he give his players appropriate verbal and non-verbal information concerning the game (see Kormelink & Seeverens, 1998b, p 11).

Second Section: Being able to read a soccer match

The coach should order match observation so that the concrete game situations are appropriately reflected in the writing, evaluation and interpretation. This should facilitate the coaching and the process of training planning and monitoring (see ibid).

Third Section: Objectives

The youth coach should set himself objectives so that he can "drive forward" the further development of his players (van Lingen, 2001, p 18).

Fourth Section: The setting of priorities

Before the start of a season, the youth coach should formulate development-specific parameters for his team and the individual players, while also orienting his training content and methods to them, depending on the playing and developmental level, via a training program with content building blocks (see ibid).

Fifth Section: Making plans

The training plans for the different content building blocks of each developmental section should be made suitably transparent and be communicated to the children and youngsters through regular coaching (comparison of current and desired states). In this way, (active) coaching becomes an effective tool for the coach in the future training and player development process. This tool should be developed on an ongoing basis together with the children and youngsters (ibid). In Dutch youth soccer, the coaching of a team and group, and of individual players, is closely linked to the *leadership style* of the youth coach. According to Trosse (2000, p21), there is a general distinction between authoritarian, *cooperative-partnership* and *laissez-faire leaderships styles*. The Dutch youth coach should, according to Spink (2001, p36), ensure that:

- the content and methods of his training and coaching

- the delegating of certain tasks to the team, the group and individuals (e.g., individual warm-up program and maintenance of the training equipment

- the monitoring of jointly established rules and standards

- the short, medium and long term objectives set by him

can be understood and reflected upon by the players on his team. Van Amstel (Jan. 28, 2003) describes this leadership style in the youth area as follows: "On paper, the cooperative-partnership style looks most effective, but the coach must be able to assess his players and ideally find a combination of all leadership styles." The identification of certain situations and the use of pedagogical aids comprise the art of the youth coach in the Netherlands.

5.3   Youth Coach Training in the KNVB

In a 2003 interview with the authors, youth coordinator and assistant coach of national league club SC Heerenveen, Henk Heising emphasized that the training of youth coaches is the key to an effective and successful, performance-oriented youth development program: "In order to develop talented players to achieve a high performance level, we need to have qualified youth coaches who have been through a high-level training program" (ibid).

Nico Romeijn, head coach at KNVB and member of the UEFA Training Committee, talks in a personal interview on Feb. 4, 2010 in Zeist about the current coach training program in the Netherlands:

Officially, every coach must start with the Trainer Coach 3 course (TC 3). He may choose whether he wants to work with junior or senior players. Then he moves on to the Trainer Coach 2 course (TC 2), which junior and senior coaches must take. Finally, there is another split in the Trainer Coach 1 course (TC 1), for juniors and seniors. (The training lasts about 1 year [author's note]). Following this is the 'Coach Betaald Voetbal' (Professional Soccer Coach). This is intended for coaches who want to work in pro soccer. (This license represents the highest qualification in Dutch soccer [author's note]).

Before the Trainer Coach 3 courses, it is possible to do several further training courses (bijscholingen) in kids' soccer, indoor soccer and/or soccer conditioning, but they are not compulsory.

In order to extend the licenses, one must obtain 12 points in five years through further education in the TC 3, TC 2 and TC 1 courses. The professional soccer coach must obtain 15 points in three years.

The content of each coaching level is naturally different. The Trainer Coach 3 course covers the match and tries to structure the training and coaching content accordingly. At the youth level, there is a more playful approach, and in the seniors, the focus is more results oriented.

The Trainer Coach 2 course teaches the development of a whole season with the focus on development/periodization/planning/evaluation. In the Trainer Coach 1 course, one mainly learns the development of a season from a coaching perspective and the development of training basiscs using pedagogical, psychological and physiological aids.

This license level, which is comparable to the UEFA A Coach license, can be completed within a period of nine months (September to May of one year) and comprises 350 teaching hours. The cost of the course is around € 6,500 ($9000) (see KNVB Academy, 2002, p 8).

All aspects of pro soccer are covered in the 'Coach Betaald Voetbal' course. The typical match scenarios of a future soccer coach are taught: match analysis, coaching, content discussions, and the question is asked again: 'How can I coach appropriately for a match?' This course includes management task material, as the coaching profession is akin to that of a manager. The 'Coach Betaald Voetbal' should not exercise the function of a manager, but learn what his job entails so that he can function in this milieu and, in particular, so that he can communicate with the 'technical director' (Nico Romeijn, Feb. 4, 2010).

Professional Soccer Coaches *(Coach Betaald Voetbal)* are awarded a nationally (1st and 2nd leagues of the KNVB) and internationally recognized license at the end of their training that qualifies them for work in elite European soccer. The course lasts one year and ends with an exam.

The *Second level - F/E/D coaching* course is intended for youth coaches. This course is composed of 12 teaching contact hours. The overall emphasis of this module is the "management and knowledge of child physiology" (KNVB Academy, 2002, p 5). The coaches of C to A juniors can do the *junior coaches* course, which consists of 30 contact hours. In addition, the International Academy of Physical Football Training (IAPF) offers youth soccer coaches in the Netherlands the possibility to do additional training in the areas of conditioning and physique. This course is not mandatory and is organized and administered by the regional associations.

The KNVB stresses that coaches at all levels make an important contribution to the learning process in Dutch youth soccer. On a positive note, the Dutch soccer coach can also manage his career independently. The free choice of activity, youth or senior soccer, at the start of one's coaching education is particularly attractive and has already been copied by many countries (e.g., Germany). In return, the KNVB requires that every club and every team manager possess a license from the association (see Peter van Amstel, 1.28.2003).

In addition, the KNVB organizes other non-mandatory coach and referee courses. The Dutch coaches training courses are particularly oriented to the practical requirements of the work of the coach at different performance levels and with different target groups (juniors and seniors). However, the Dutch training system remains very transparent and flexible as both senior and junior coaches can change track by attending the appropriate courses. It is therefore quite common in the Netherlands for senior coaches to change and become junior coaches or vice versa.

5.4 The KNVB Soccer Academy

The KNVB has worldwide recognition and is responsible for training, education and innovation in youth, amateur and professional soccer in the Netherlands. Dutch coaching licenses are recognized by UEFA.

In the 1960s, training programs for trainers *(oefenmeester)* were run in Zeist, from which evolved the terms *trainer* and *coach*. In 1984, Rinus Michels led the Academy as Technical Director and National Team Coach *(Bondscoach)* and carried out significant changes:

- Changes in the training of coaches and referees

- Restructuring of youth coaching

- Youth coaching as an ongoing task for the future

In 1996, the KNVB Academy was founded. It is recognized in the Netherlands as the institute for national and international training programs and detailed analysis. The KNVB Academy, in cooperation with the six regional associations *(districts)*, runs about 600 courses annually, attended by about 12,000 coaches. The KNVB Academy has a separate department that is able to concentrate exclusively on international projects (see KNVB Academy, 2010b), which enables the KNVB to offer courses to coaches, soccer associations and other organizations from all over the world that conform to the Dutch *Zeister Vision* in terms of content and methodology.

The KNVB Academy also develops and releases DVDs, CD-ROMs and videos, e-learning programs and textbooks about and for Dutch soccer.

The KNVB Academy training program is very diverse, reacts to innovations and can be seen online at any time (see KNVB Academy, 2010c):

Trainer / Coach training for all levels

- UEFA C/Trainer-Coach III (TC III) Seniors
- UEFA C/Trainer-Coach III (TC III) Jeugd (Juniors)
- UEFA B/Trainer-Coach II (TC II)
- UEFA A/Trainer-Coach I (TC I) Seniors
- UEFA A/Trainer-Coach I (TC I) Jeugd (Juniors)
- UEFA Pro/Coach Betaald Voetbal (CBV) soccer coach
- Trainer Coach Zaalvoetbal III (Indoor soccer 3)
- Trainer Coach Zaalvoetbal II (Indoor soccer 2)
- Bijscholing/"Ontwikkelen van een speelwijze" (Training/development of playing style)

Training for Volunteers

- Youth leader
- Module F Youth coach
- Module E Youth coach
- Module D Youth coach
- Children's coach
- Junior coach
- Technical youth coordinator 2
- Technical youth coordinator 3
- G-soccer coach
- Goalkeeping coach level 2/Basic goalkeeping coaches course
- Goalkeeping coach level 3/Advanced goalkeeping coaches course

Training for Referees

- Children's referees
- Juniors' referees
- Basic training for soccer referees
- Basic training for indoor soccer referees
- Short Basic referee training course

- Short Basic indoor referee training course

- Referee 2 field

- Referee 2 indoor

- Referee 1 field

- Referee 1 indoor

- Assistant referee

- Attendant referee/field/Futsal

Management Pro Soccer

Soccer Development Programs

Workshops and Seminars

Coaching Seminars and Symposia

Readings

Advanced Soccer and Futsal Training

Administrative Soccer Seminars

In order to allow the KNVB Academy to become even more transparent and communicative, the KNVB Online Academy was founded at the end of 2009 (see KNVB Academy, 2010). The benefits of an online academy are:

- The exchange of ideas

- The experience of desires and criticisms

- Offering electronic learning programs

- Sets of rules for referees and commentators for field soccer and Futsal

- Final exams for courses via online tests

The KNVB's very comprehensive and thoroughly differentiated coaching and training program shows exactly why so many international soccer associations and soccer schools draw on its contents and methods, central ideas, unique innovations and structural elements of Dutch soccer education.

6 Playing, Coaching and Training Philosophies in the Netherlands

"Playing simple soccer is the most difficult thing of all. That is the problem of all coaches. How often do you see a 40m pass when 20m would have been sufficient, or a double pass in the penalty area when seven players are standing around you, while a simple lateral pass around the seven men would have simplified everything. The obvious, simple solution seems to be the hardest of all to implement."

(Johan Cruyff, Vrij Nederland, December 1974; quoted in Barend & van Dorp, 2006, p 22)

Coaching in the Netherlands is generally considered by most of those responsible in soccer as a kind of ongoing collaborative process between individuals. Therefore, in the Netherlands, there is no *strict* separation between youth and senior training (see the interview with Huub Stevens in Chapter 6.3). Louis van Gaal used the noun *process* regularly in the German media. When interviewed about a victory, draw or defeat of his team, he always links the isolated incident with his ongoing *holistic* training work with the team in collaboration with his coaching and support staff. In this way, many successful Dutch pro soccer coaches are building a bridge into the *future* because they know that changes and improvements through training and interactions with people take time (see ibid). This approach regularly causes irritation when voiced in the German media. The (expected) quick success in the professional senior game is at odds with the future-oriented, process-driven Dutch professional playing, coaching and training philosophies. According to Kormelink and Seeverens (2002, p 5), the process-driven nature of training and coaching is based on the principle that high performance-oriented training can only be undertaken after a preliminary analysis of training sessions, matches and personal chats with the players. This principle is also transferred to youth development soccer in the Netherlands. The coaches in the different age groups should communicate intensively with each other *before* the selection of coaching methods and contents to enable a structured and well thought out coaching program that develops players to a professional standard. In the Netherlands, the future-oriented order, perspective and goal-setting of youth training (preparation to be a professional player) is linked to an ongoing interaction and communication *process* (first and second order cybernetics). What does this future-oriented training look like in detail? What is the vision?

6.1   The Zeist Vision[10] in Youth Soccer

When something that exists now is projected into the future, it is usually referred to in Dutch as a Vision. According to Zeist Vision, talented young players should be coached so that, in the future, many players pursue the sport of soccer at all performance levels (see van Lingen, 2001, p 35). The Dutch training philosophy is closely linked to this objective.

Youth training should ensure both the optimization of performance and enjoyment of the game: "When soccer training is made simple" players learn "to play soccer!" easier (ibid, p 38). This is why young Dutch players have been guided by the model of street soccer for decades. According to Michels, the traditional street training games should be reproduced in club training because "these forms are what real soccer is all about" (ibid, 2000a, p 147). Here Michels refers to the many constant repetitions of techniques and play situations in street soccer (and its variants). The Zeist Vision rejects training in isolation and is in favor of simple games and training games in particularly for kids. Street soccer is therefore "broken down" into small training games in the Netherlands. The playing philosophy of soccer is central to youth coaching regarding scoring and preventing goals. This philosophy, which proceeds primarily from an implicit learning process, places particular demands on the club coach. In the Netherlands, he is not considered a kind of "physical instructor," but a coach in the sense of an advisor, counselor and mentor of the young players (see Kraif, 2007 and Chapter 5.2). This objective and task-oriented coaching represents the key difference to "free and non-pressurized" street soccer, meaning the situations in a training game is the "question" for the player, and the technical-tactical solution is the playing "answer."

The Zeist Vision is a methodology in which the desired learning effects can be achieved via motivating training games: "Every player shows his true face when playing soccer" (van Lingen, 2001, p 36). According to Mariman (2002b, p. 32), the Zeist Vision represents a method in the training process that primarily involves competitive soccer-specific forms, small-sided games and team-oriented positional play: "In a match, man always plays against man; he doesn't run around cones. For this reason, we always train in a match-typical way" (Dusseldorp, Seeverens & Vergoossen, 2000).

---

10   This vision is formulated by the KNVB. The association is headquartered in the city of Zeist near Utrecht.

The Zeist Vision tries to copy the type of match that finds its particular expression in street soccer. In the Netherlands, the Zeist Vision is not uncontested. In some clubs, the development of "soccer performance" (van Lingen, 2001, p 38) is supplemented by isolated technique training with the aid of drills (see the Coerver Method in Chapter 7.3), so that in the training process, hybrid forms exist that combine the use of drills and training games (see Mariman, 2002b, p 30).[11]

---

11   At this point, the interested reader is directed to the international research work of Roth (2000), Raab, Hossner and Memmert on technique and tactics training and to the "Heidelberg Ball School" in the ball games of Memmert (2006) and Thumfart (2006) on "Optimal Tactics Training in Youth and High Performance Soccer." They are intellectual building blocks for the analysis and structure of learning processes in youth soccer and represent links to Chapter 6.1.2 in terms of content and methodology.

6.1.1 The KNVB Training Methodology

The KNVB divides the methodology of youth training into six sections, which coaches should respect when it comes to talent development.

In the **first section**, children and juniors should be taught the four main phases of soccer:

1. Ball possession
2. Switching on losing the ball
3. Opponent's ball possession
4. Switching on winning the ball

In order to illustrate the first section in practical terms, in the ensuing **second section**, the 11- a side match is broken down into small-sided team games (2v2, 3v3, 4v4, 7v7, etc.).

In the **third section**, the youth coach should look for and develop training games whose objectives, time, space, functions and tasks may be changed (see van Lingen, 2001, p 39). These elements confront the children and juniors with constantly changing game situations in training that contribute to the development of independently achieved solution patterns.

In the **fourth section**, the positive and negative developments within the team in the context of the TIC model (see Chapter 4.2.1) should be analyzed and addressed in a soccer-specific manner in training. That means that, in this section, the elements of technique training, communication and playful intelligence are priorities in the development of talented young players.

In the **fifth section**, coaches offer many game and exercise forms (e.g., goals must be scored using the head, only two ball touches are allowed, etc.) in different situations to allow for training games with even (from 2v2 to 9v9) and uneven-sided teams. With this approach, youth players experience a match-appropriate training structure as the arrangements allow for differing pressure components in time, accuracy, variability and complexity.

In the **sixth section**, the *big match* should be emulated: 11v11 taking all impediments and solutions into consideration, which allow the youth coach to identify regression or progress in the development of all the players by observation (see van Lingen, 2001, p 39; KNVB Academy, 2010e).

The key element of this stage of the Zeist Vision is the constant confrontation of the youth player with the type of problems that arise in matches and which he should be able to solve based on the foundation of the TIC model.

According to KNVB ideology, the concrete structure of a training session should be split into three phases:

1. Orientation
2. Practice and learning
3. Implementation (see Petersen, 2001, p 24)

In training, each phase flows naturally into the next. Each training session starts with a warm-up (first phase) and usually consists of running, stretching, positional play and passing. In the *orientation phase*, the focus should be on positional play in which the players can consolidate and implement their techniques in a varied and creative manner (e.g., passing and dribbling). In addition, match situations with a predominantly group-tactical emphasis are simulated and should reproduce the different pressure situations. In the *practice and learning phase*, the training emphasis lies on the players' match-typical behavior patterns: "what can I play in this spot (e.g., pass into a space or dribble forward and shot on goal) and how can I effectively resolve a match situation (e.g., 'hard flat pass' or 'fast dribbling and shot on goal with the toe')? The tactical pressure on the players increases, for as well as the match simulation, positional changes and team-tactical tasks under opponent pressure are also included!" (Edward Sturing, March 13, 2003). In the *implementation phase*, the training focus is on the target 11v11 form, in which the first two phases should be visible in a "free game." Within this phase, the youth coach can also allow team-tactical elements, such as wing play, pressing or counterattacking, to be incorporated or developed. At the end of a training session planned in this way, set pieces (e.g., corners and free kicks) are often practiced, and it is concluded with a slow jog (see Petersen, 2001, p 24).

6.1.2 The Importance of Game Training in Dutch Youth Soccer

The above explanations of the Dutch soccer development system indicate that games and training games dominate in this coaching philosophy.

The 11v11 game is usually split into small-sided games. Horst Wein (2001, p 10), an expert in particular on Dutch, Spanish and German soccer, cites the importance of games and playing for kid's and youth soccer as follows: "playing games is as vital for children as sleep. Playing is necessary for the health of their bodies and minds." The KNVB's approach goes beyond these generally prominent and key components of playing and the game, and opposes the dominance of practicing techniques in isolation:

"it isn't just about learning technical skills, but about learning functional technical skills" (Mariman, 2002a, p 21). Soccer should therefore be trained in a match-like training game.

According to Mariman, technique training can also be organized in a playful way. When practicing isolated technique forms, the following rules should be observed: "forms that include opponents are prioritized, if there is little training time available – more forms with opponents should be practiced and the technique should always be seen functionally" (ibid, p 22). The selected training games should be grouped according to training emphasis, whose objective is the improvement of defensive (e.g., behavior in zonal defense and when pressing) and offensive players (e.g., shifting the game, wing play, ball retention, playing without the ball, counterattacking). Different combinations for training offensive and defensive play can be practiced in tackling training or uneven-sided games.

6.1.3   The Dutch 4v4 Training Game Form in Theory and Practice

It is consistent with the Dutch conception of soccer that children in particular really love to compete against each other in play. Children should develop their own solutions in open play situations. Playing in small spaces with many ball contacts and frequent 1 on 1 situations is consistent with this concept and the following soccer-specific coaching goals:

*   Improvement of technical ability and skills (passing, shooting, dribbling)

*   Using playing space and time, and opponent pressure for the development of tactical behavior (combine in all playing directions, so that it is possible to play wide and deep [see van Lingen & Pauw, 2001b, p 19])

*   Possibilities to transfer learned technical-tactical abilities and skills into the target 11v11 game (see van der Meer, 2000, p 11)

The 4v4 game (plus two goalkeepers) also reflects the Zeist Vision and the vision of the TIC model and, according to van der Meer (ibid, p 13), follows three objectives:

*   Retention of ball possession even when the opponent is hassling you

*   Being able to dribble the ball well

*   Being able to score goals quickly

These objectives are put into practice in the following selected 4v4 small-sided games *(partij-spelletjes)*[12] in Dutch youth training:

---

12   The illustrations below are partly explained by a language that corresponds to the jargon of modern pro soccer coaches and players. They are therefore very authentic in terms of training work on the pitch and are not put into formal language. The small-sided games can be adapted for all age-groups, so the authors deliberately give no specific advice here.

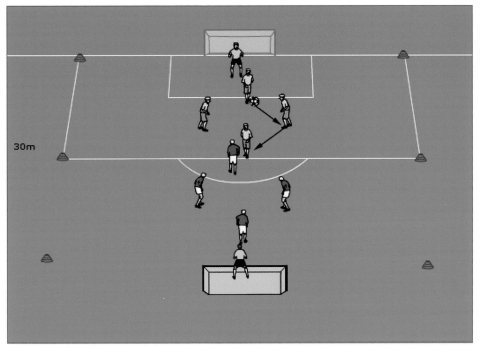

Fig. 1: 4v4 with two wide goals with two goalkeepers

Procedure

- Two teams (A and B) play on a 30m x 30m pitch into two wide goals with goal-keepers.

- Both teams play in 1-2-1 formation.

- Both teams may only play flat passes. As soon as the ball is kicked too high, the opposing team gets a penalty (i.e., one player from one team plays 1v1 against the goalkeeper of the other team).

Coaching

- "Always try to form triangles."

- Make sure that players adopt optimal positions on the pitch and control the distances between each other.

- Play toward the goal and look for the quickest route to the goal.

Variations

- Play with one ball touch (at higher levels).

- Allow 1-2 touches.

- Mark out zones on the pitch to help the players orient themselves.

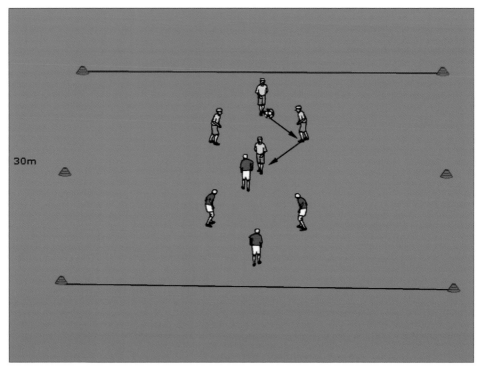

Fig. 2: 4v4 with line dribbling

Procedure

- See Fig. 1, but this time, dribbling over the opposing team's line counts as a goal.
- Both teams should again only play flat passes.
- Again, play in a 1-2-1 formation.

Coaching

- Avoid unnecessary dribbling: "play as a team."
- Prepare scoring chances carefully.
- Ask the forward to play decisively and creatively 1 on 1.

Variations

- Mark out half of the pitch with cones, and only score goals into the left or right halves.
- Score a goal within a certain time (time pressure).
- Play 3v4 or 4v3.

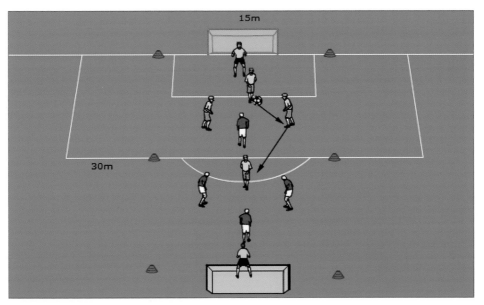

Fig. 3: 4v4 on a long, narrow pitch

Procedure

- See Fig. 1
- The pitch is 40m long and 10-15m wide.
- Passes should be flat.
- Every team has a limit of three high and mid-height passes. If this limit is exceeded, a penalty is awarded.

Coaching

- "Think" deep (play stab passes).
- Precise and variable positional play in a narrow space as preparation for the "long ball."
- Fast "1-2" combinations.
- Ensure coordinated teamwork between the player kicking the ball and the "deep" players.

Variations

- Work with one center line; for example, if the ball crosses this line, it may not be played back into the rear half of the pitch.
- The attackers must score the goals.
- Limit the number of ball touches, according to ability.

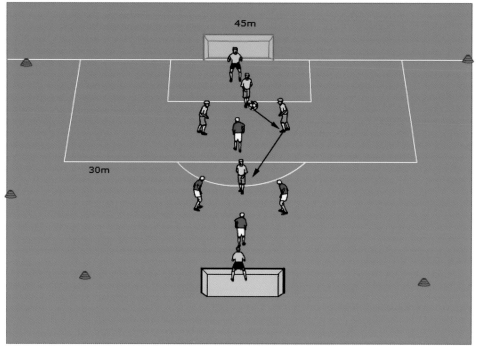

Fig. 4: 4v4 on a wide pitch (with wing play and centering of the ball)

Procedure

- See Fig. 1: play into two big goals with goalkeepers.
- The size of the pitch is changed so that it is 30m long and 45m wide.
- Now add centering the ball so that not only flat balls count.

Coaching

- Watch out for the "offensive" header (one-footed take-off).
- The "wingers" can play without restrictions.
- High centered passes near the goal must be caught by the goalkeeper.

Variations

- Mark out a 6m-wide wing zone in which the "center passer" may not be tackled.
- Headed goals count double.
- When the "defensive" headed ball is won, the winning team is also awarded a penalty kick *(strafschop)*.

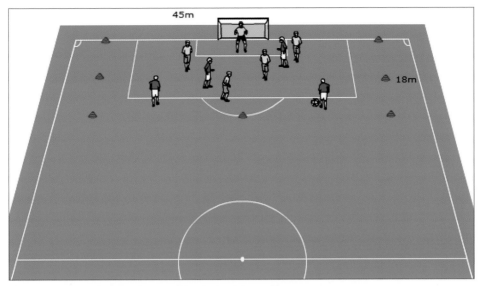

Fig. 5: 4v4 on a short and very wide pitch with goalkeeper

Procedure

- See Fig. 4, but the pitch is now 18m long and 45m wide.

- Team A plays into a wide goal and keeper. Team B plays into a 45m wide line marked with cones.

Coaching

- Ball possession by team A

  - Precise and variable position play with fast ball pace.

  - Aim for "quick" 1-2s along the width of the pitch.

  - Deliberately interrupt combinations and involve the goalkeeper in the game.

- Ball possession by team B

  - Precise passing forward of the ball.

  - Dribble into open spaces.

  - Do not allow team A to counterattack.

Variations

- Team A should only play with 1-2 touches.

- Team A should only use flat passes.

- Team B should play into two wide goals with goalkeepers who stand next to each other in the wide goal.

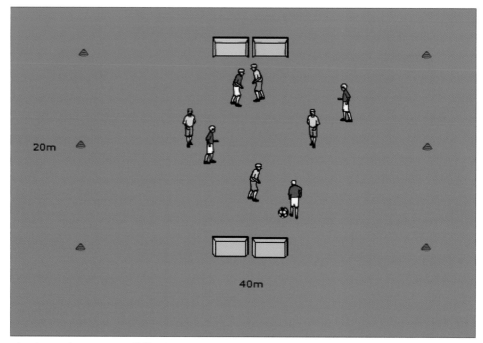

Fig. 6: 4v4 into two small "ice hockey goals"

Procedure
- Play on a 40m x 20m pitch into two small ice hockey goals that are placed centrally.
- Play in 1-2-1 formation.

Coaching
- As soon as no defensive playing foot of the opposing player can be seen, shoot into the empty ice hockey goal.
- "Think deep, play deep."
- The complete order is retained with the ball and against the ball

Variations
- Both ice hockey goals are staggered one behind the other.
- The pitch is halved down the center. If the ball is passed into the offensive side, it is passed back.
- Play 5v3.

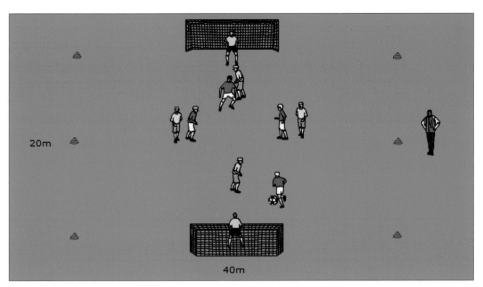

Fig. 7: 4v4 with time pressure

Procedure

- See Fig. 6, but play into two wide goals with goalkeepers.
- Pitch size is 40m x 20m.
- The coach determines both teams' results. If team A is losing 0:1, they get the ball and 3 minutes in which to score a goal.
- The losing team must attack and press while playing a 3-1 system.
- The winning team should keep the ball.

Coaching

- The losing team should attack the players with the ball and, in particular, block passes down the center.
- The winning team should try to use the width of the pitch.
- Both teams should play aggressively (pressure to succeed).

Variations

- If the losing team scores a goal, it counts double.
- Set the score at 0:0 and then hold a sudden-death play-off. The team that scores first wins.
- Set the score at 0:0. As soon as one team scores, this team loses a player (Gladiator game).

Fig. 8: 4v4 with three teams

Procedure

- Play into two wide goals with goalkeepers on a 40m x 20m pitch.

- Team A plays against team B. Team C stands behind A's goal.

- As soon as A loses the ball, team B plays against C. Team A then stands behind B's goal. If B loses the ball, C plays against A.

- The team that wins the ball first passes the ball 3 times among its own players. The opponents are passive in this phase, thus allowing the build-up of an ordered attack (avoid chaos).

Coaching

- Fast switching by all teams.

- Be alert during the entire playing process.

- Avoid hectic moves; chances should be prepared precisely with combination play.

Variations

- Switch without the team holding onto the ball.

- Vary the number of ball touches.

- The players must shoot on goal within a certain time limit.

Internationally, 4v4 games are now ubiquitous in children's and youths' training. In addition, tournaments and matches can also be played on 35m x 25m pitches (see Hyballa, 2001b, p 10). They are easy to organize because user-friendly application software is available. Compared to the 3v3 preferred by von Wein (2004, p 30-13), the 4v4 allows play in the full width and depth of the pitch. However, the importance of uneven-sided games to improve combination play in children's and youths' soccer is not included in the Dutch youth philosophy of the 4v4.

6.2 Dominant and Offensive – the Playing and Training Philosophy of Louis van Gaal

German Champion and Cup Winner 2010 and Champions League Finalist 2010)[13]

In order to be able to authentically describe the training philosophy of Louis van Gaal, the authors have translated an interview with van Gaal (2006, pps 4-16) in the technical publication *TrainersMagazine*. The soccer coach of German national league club SC Freiburg, Robin Dutt, explains the playing and training philosophy of Louis van Gaal in the form of a comparison as follows in an interview with *Kicker Magazine*: "Van Gaal prefers a variable offensive game with good dribblers of the ball on the wing. Barcelona plays a variable offensive game in which the players switch positions. Both are successful, but their philosophies are different." (ibid, quoted in Röser, 2010, 29). In this interview, van Gaal explains his understanding of the frequently used terms *dominant and offensive* soccer. The translation of the interview is presented below:

Playing dominant soccer in van Gaal's opinion means creating more goal-scoring opportunities than the other team. For van Gaal, offensive soccer is linked to a very high technical and tactical ability, along with an absolute will to win. He always distinguishes between a more offensive and less defensive playing formation. According to van Gaal, players must always decide for themselves what happens on the pitch, which is understandably a topic that is open to discussion for him. If the team plays using a defensive playing system, it also has a certain approach, which ensures that the opposing team can only attack into a small space. The coach does not see this approach as dominant because the playing situation is not offensive.

Dominant

Whether wanting to play dominant soccer always means playing in the opposing team's half is also open to discussion for van Gaal. For example, PSV Eindhoven's game can be called dominant as they win a lot of matches. However, the players tend to do this from

---

13 In his new two-part book *Biografie & Visie*, Louis van Gaal (2010b) describes in great detail his personal development and his vision of soccer.

a defensive formation and so do not correspond to van Gaal's criteria. "PSV always play very compact and well-organized soccer. This means playing dominantly in a different sense of the word. *I link the term dominant with offensive soccer and pressing in the other team's half.* I also choose to play like this because we are always trying to excite the public. If you play offensive soccer, the fans are entertained. If you play more passively, you are only occasionally dominant. I think that the fans prefer to watch offensive soccer."

Winning Titles

"If you want to play dominant soccer, then a little depends on the other team's quality but particularly yours matters." Van Gaal remembers the words of van Basten, when he was appointed Dutch National Coach (*Bondscoach*). He had also tried to get his team to play dominant soccer, but it wasn't always possible at that level. The intention, the idea, may always have been there, but it was the qualities of the players that were decisive. "There are excellent coaches who are not that well-known. They can boast great success and get the best performances out of a group. The public doesn't see this though as the teams don't win cups or championships. But this is only possible with the most talented players. If you have constantly worked at the highest level, it is easier to win a title."

Confidence

Of course, there are also coaches who work at the very highest levels and who let their opponents take the initiative. According to van Gaal, this is another type of approach. "If you want to play a waiting game, you not only need a different type of player, but also a completely different philosophy. The coaching is different and a different type of player is scouted. In the Netherlands, we coach all players according to an offensive concept. If all these players were allowed to play defensively, it would be a difficult change to make. Everybody knows that Ajax Amsterdam can be put under pressure because they have not been coached for this and therefore have problems with it."

Playing dominant soccer has a lot to do with **confidence**, and requires good players and confidence in the ability of those players to play dominant soccer. In a group, there are many things that can be influenced by this. If one wants good results, one must take this into consideration. Whether one ultimately wants to play dominantly is determined by the players, technical staff, medical staff, officials and, of course, the fans and media. In the very top clubs, this is much harder to handle than in van Gaal's former club, AZ Alkmaar. "When I was signed to AZ, the thinking in this club changed immediately. They were, in theory, still just below the top (*subtopper*), but the media paid much more attention to the club."

Mental

"The product of soccer is influenced by the interaction between the players and the technical and medical staff. The most important thing is the quality of the players, closely followed by the quality of the coach. I think that the coach has a huge influence." When van Gaal was at AZ Alkmaar, the team was not well-balanced. For example, there were three right wingers but only one left-winger. The mental quality of the players was good though and they got along well together. "We had a squad that worked hard, which is very important."

Formation

The formation used by a team has a big influence on the way it plays. Louis van Gaal has used a 1-4-3-3 formation for years, but he does vary it. "If you play 1-4-3-3, I believe you have an ideal pitch coverage. It is open to discussion whether in the center you play with the point forward or backward. Many teams currently play with the point backward, although I prefer the point forward, because if you push through a player from behind, there is more space there for him" (see Fig. 9 and 10 [author's note]).

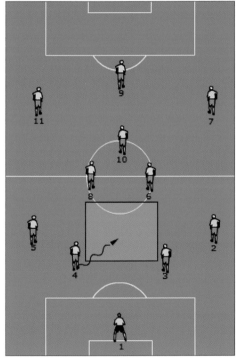
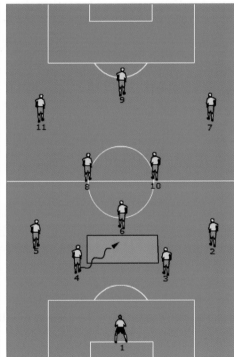

Fig. 9: 1-4-3-3 formation with point (number 10) forward

Fig. 10: 1-4-3-3 formation with point (number 6) backward

"More space is automatically created to push from behind."

"When playing with the point backward, space must be created somewhere by running. That is a small, but very important point. I also believe that, in general, when playing with the point backward, the strikers are too far away.

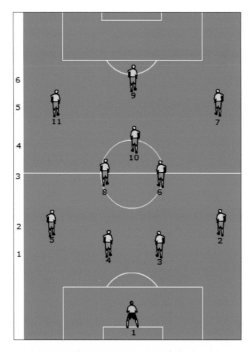

Fig. 11: 1-4-3-3 formation with point (number 10) forward and six lines (numbers 1-6 in the margin of the illustration)

This often makes the point too isolated. It depends on the quality of the midfield players whether he can connect or not." Van Gaal thinks that choice of formation always depends on the group of players available. A formation must be chosen according to the quality of the playing group. "The good thing about the formation we use is that we create a large number of lines. If you play 1-4-4-2 with a flat 4, then you have only three or four lines. In our formation, we play with six lines" (see Fig. 11 [author's note]). "Looked at from a mathematical point of view, this creates a lot more passing possibilities. This pitch coverage allows both better attack and better defense."

Defense

"In this formation, there is always a player who can put the ball under pressure. When players are standing next to each other, it is easier for the opponent to run free with a couple of back passes (see Fig. 12).

A player must then stand vertically in order to resolve this, which takes time so that the opponent has time to play the pass, and you are always too late to stop him. If the players are standing next to each other, from a mathematical point of view, it is much harder to put the opponent under pressure, as one player must always run out of this formation. If other lines are available (see Fig. 11), it is easier to 'surround' the opponent. There

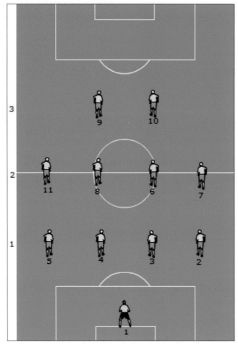

Fig. 12: 1-4-4-2-formation/system and three lines

are also zones that must be covered. For example, take FC Barcelona, who play with the point backward in the midfield. They push right over to one side and leave the other side completely free. If you press well on the ball though, it doesn't come on the other side. Pressing only works if you have good field coverage. The more lines you have, the better you can 'surround' and build up pressure on the ball." For van Gaal, the distance between the players is very important when pressing. The players who are farthest from the ball must come right in. All players must be ready to do something. The many lines create distance between the players no greater than 5m to10m. For van Gaal, this makes it easier for the players to run.

Opponent

The opponent's formation does not greatly influence your own game. "Our pitch coverage is always the same. That means that the players must run less. If the opponent plays with four defenders, the left-winger, for example, can come in slightly, in order to provoke a pass to the other team's right half, thereby restoring the team's own order. The opponent then no longer has numerical superiority. If the opposing opening player runs into the center, the point can remain with the other central defender and thus force him to win possession of the ball. Again, I feel that the distances are so small that the opponent can be put under pressure." According to van Gaal, these things always depend upon the qualities of both the team and its opponents. The opponent must be lured in and then the ball guided to where you want to gain possession of it. Previous analysis will reveal how the opponents prefer to build their game. "It can be that we tie up the opponent by pushing forward the number 10, so that we play 1 on 1 on the whole pitch."

Long Ball

According to van Gaal, many clubs decide to play "long balls" to immediately send the "problem" into the opponent's half. "I always try to get my team to resolve the build-up by playing. If you use long balls, the team must be organized differently. If you know this, the team must also have a different mental approach. If this happens, you must be careful that you have a second man where the ball lands. Then, tactically, you have to ensure that one more player is available in this space. The players must be mentally prepared for this in order to fight for the second ball."

Van Gaal says that the same is also true for the moment when the opponent kicks the long ball, that there must also be enough players around the ball and the defenders must adapt to it. "It's not about the players, it's not about the ball; it's about covering the space into which the ball is kicked better than the opponent. When you know how the opponent plays the long ball, the team must be trained so that the defenders can cover the space behind it better than the other team's forward at the front."

Offensive

According to van Gaal, the offensive style of play is also connected to the defensive style of play. He explains this by pointing out that creating lines is important for successful positional play. "If you play fast, circulation soccer, you can put the opponent under pressure. If you always pass the ball around, the opponent must also always spread out. The chance is then greater that the opponent will make positional errors. If a player stands still or dribbles slowly, the opponent can defend better. If you stand still for two seconds, every opposing player has time to correct any positional errors. If a player suddenly decides to dribble fast, the opponent has no time to correct his mistake. A problem then arises if the other team stands so compactly that the ball must also be passed wide and is therefore easier to defend." Van Gaal likes to use the terms *ball distribution* and *ball circulation*. "Ball distribution doesn't mean that you can't dribble. You must know the moment when you can create a 2v1 situation by dribbling. If the opponent manages to attack the player with the ball with back-up, then don't dribble, otherwise you'll end up in a 1v2 situation."

Creative Players

"The attacking party must ensure that the creative players make space so that at critical moments they can dribble or make an action. These players have the chance to create something. Other players do not possess these qualities." In order to put creative players in a situation where they can perform, player types are needed who can quickly pass the ball on. According to van Gaal, creative players have a certain window of time in a certain zone in which to make the difference in a match. "Creative players can also push forward with more or less risk in a small space. If you then also have midfielders who can make the right choices in a small space, this is an advantage for you as a coach."

Position Changes

Van Gaal believes that position changes are not the way to outplay a compact defense. "If an opponent defends compactly, and we change positions, they are still standing there. When the ball is played, they will then attack you (at least, if it is a good opponent). Against average opponents, it can work. I think that a player must work from a certain position. This position is not linked to a certain line. This position is about a zone in which a player can and must play. For the left-winger, for example, it is the space between the penalty area and the center line on the corresponding side of the pitch. He must see this space in relation to his teammates and his opponents. From this space, he must create space for his teammates but also at the right time close the space up again. He must learn to start from this specific position out of a preliminary action to create space for himself. This happens the moment the ball arrives. You train this by passing to him under opponent pressure, and also by involving a third player. It can be coached in exercise forms and small-sided games."

Training Drills *(Oefenstof)*

Van Gaal hints that he is no fan of books of exercise forms. His coaching is based on an objective according to which he develops exercise forms. "The players must play positional play from their position. If they get some space, they learn to operate in this space and automatically to communicate with their teammates and opponents. We then say, for example, that position 11 in positional play may only stand in zones 1 and 2, so that every player plays from his position.

If we now include the goalkeeper, the build-up can be practiced. The coach must be creative in these areas. You can also only pass to the right, to the left or over a certain line." Van Gaal is not interested in exercise forms but in objectives. The objective must create the exercise forms. "I think up exercise forms from the match situation. I see what a player does well or badly in each situation and then I coach it."

Success

"To acheive success, you must be mentally tough. A team must learn to win. It takes time to get a team to feel that it is unbeatable. If they lose, they must be revitalized again. If a team loses too often, they lose the automatic winning feeling."

Louis van Gaal can look back on an outstanding success story at Ajax. PSV Eindhoven could have written a similar success story a few years ago with Guus Hiddink. Van Gaal is interested in everything. For him, the details determine the system and vice versa.

6.3 Detail and Technique-oriented: The Playing, Coaching and Training Philosophy of Huub Stevens
(Austrian Champion 2010)

Huub Stevens joins the long tradition of Dutch players and soccer coaches (*Coach Betaald Voetbal*) who were already coaching youth teams during their time as players. Huub Stevens did this while at PSV Eindhoven. Also during this time, he worked through the KNVB coaching course. What was the significance of youth soccer for Huub Stevens in his different careers as player and soccer coach? What are the secrets of success of Dutch youth soccer? What is his opinion of modern German youth soccer? In the interview below (conducted with him on Jan. 19, 2010) he answers all these questions.

Huub Stevens
(born November 29, 1953 in Sittard)
18-time Dutch national player
Played for Fortuna Sittard and PSV Eindhoven,
soccer coach at PSV Eindhoven
(Juniors and Seniors)
Roda Kerkrade
Schalke 04
Hertha BSC Berlin
1. FC Cologne
Hamburger SV and
Austrian Champion 2010
with Red Bull Salzburg

Authors: *Mr. Stevens, please tell us how you became a coach.*

HS: During my pro career, first at Fortuna Sittard and later at PSV Eindhoven, I was always interested in youth soccer. As a player, I always watched youth matches when I had time, for that was where real soccer was played. I liked it! In my last two years as a player, I coached the U15s at PSV, and when my playing career finished, I became youth coordinator at PSV. In addition, I gradually completed my coaching license and educated myself up to the highest diploma, the *Coach Betaald Voetball* (professional soccer coach).

Authors: *So that's why your first coaching post was with a youth team. In hindsight, how important and instructive was this time for you?*

HS: Very important for me personally. Coaching is learned by working from the bottom up, to allow your "coaching eye" to develop. In youth soccer, the most important thing is the development of individual players, and as a coach, you are responsible for special detailed training. In technique training in particular, you take care of every detail. For example, does the youngster receive the ball with the right or left foot? Based on this, you develop many things for bilateral play, etc. You learn to coach very well in youth soccer, as a good player does not necessarily make a good coach. You must learn many things, such as patience in training, how to keep calm, how to talk in front of a group and explain technical things so that young people can actually understand them! Youth soccer is a great experimental field, but it's what you make of it yourself that is important. As a young player, I was just as motivated as I was later in pro soccer! Even today, as a pro coach, I still watch what is going on in youth soccer because that's where the foundations are laid, and as a pro coach, you absolutely benefit from how the youth coaches work. Pro coaches should never forget that!

Authors: In your opinion, *what is the main difference between youth and senior soccer?*

HS: The big difference quite clearly lies in development. In youth soccer, you must develop, develop and develop again! You must help on individual players. In pro soccer, what counts is match day, and winning the game; the performance of the team and results-oriented success. In youth soccer, I believe that we shouldn't work so much on tactics, but on technique and coordination. You need to continuously set the juniors tasks that they can solve. For example, if you play against a weak opponent, then as coach, you must deliberately encourage the players only to play with 1-2 contacts. Attractive combination soccer promotes and requires these measures. Even if it means that results suffer. It's important for the learning process. That's all that matters in youth soccer!

Authors: *Why do you think Dutch youth soccer is so successful?*

HS: I think that in the Netherlands, we are very detail-oriented in certain learning phases. In children's soccer, there is a lot of playing, but really only focusing on coordination and technique. By this I mean that in the 5-8 age group, we focus quite a lot on physical coordination, and in the 8-12 age group on ball technique and more advanced physical coordination. We work a lot with the Coerver Method, so a lot (of time is spent) in the areas of coordination and technique. A player must always concentrate on these areas. Dutch youth coaches then want to see these Coerver movements again and again in the small sided games. So not just scoring goals in the games but before shooting on goal, the players must also show certain moves that have previously been practiced. In the older youth area, positional play drills (*positiespel*) are introduced, in which the players must demonstrate appropriate technical patterns from their specific positions. Consequently, the passing game must be trained again and again with the aid of many different, appropriate passing drills. The player is taught in different game situations what he can do better and more creatively on the pitch. However, one secret of Dutch youth soccer is certainly also the fact that Dutch youth soccer coaches have a quite pedantic attention to detail!

Authors: *Please explain the Dutch "secret of youth soccer" and can you perhaps use certain "magic words?"*

HS: One magic word is definitely future *(Toekomst)*. Everything that is done in the youth area must be future-oriented. Of course, it is nice to win a C junior championship, but that is just temporary, and every youth coach must know that. It is important that everyone is able to identify with the future. You must always see your work in perspective, which is why the youth coaches must all communicate well with each other and each one must be taken seriously. The A junior coach is not more important than the D junior coach. Both have different demands and tasks, and must fulfill them. The A junior coach must have a more adult way of talking to the players and have good knowledge of positional tactics. The D junior coach's approach must be a friendlier one, and he should be an absolute expert in the areas of dribbling, passing and the development of creative ideas. He must also be able to constantly motivate the players. But both must understand and ensure that the players enjoy training and playing, and both must be able to rely on each other in a club. As I said, it's also nice to win matches, but a coach should not be judged by this criterion.

In youth soccer, we must make sure that Dutch players are equipped with loads of creative ideas. Losing is part of the process, and for me it's more important than winning, as it can be worked on together and players can learn far more from it!

Authors: *You have worked as a coach in both the Netherlands and Germany. What do you think is the biggest difference in youth soccer between the two countries?*

HS: I think it's fantastic that the German U17, U19 and U21 teams have all become European champions. The players and coaches must always stretch themselves, but even these titles are only temporary. Nobody can say that it is so important to win junior titles. Let me clarify; titles are important, but the coaching and how it is conducted, is 100 times more important! Whether a super 14-year-old player will still be a super 16-year-old player is the most important thing. Titles can quickly breed complacency and allow juniors to get ahead of themselves. In Germany, young players are built up as stars much too soon. You must not pay too much attention to pure results. Only the coaching content counts.

I think that in Germany, too many German youth coaches emphasize **the will to win**. They should concentrate more on how to improve passing, dribbling and certain training contents.

When I was head coach at FC Schalke 04, I saw how teams from the D and C juniors went for runs in the woods on Mondays. I don't think this is a good idea. Young players want the ball and should have the ball. You can only play creative soccer if you master the appropriate ball techniques. To learn this, young players do not need to go running; they need the ball! That is what matters! I also think that in Germany, soccer is very much based on running ability, and this philosophy starts at the youth level. In the Netherlands, we are more interested in how to resolve a game situation and how creativity can be used without having to use a lot of energy and running. Perhaps this sometimes looks a little elaborate in the game, but you can only develop ideas by moving the ball and your body with a lot of creative skill.

In Germany, they use lactate tests a lot, but they don't exist in the Netherlands. We play a different kind of soccer. Good fitness is important, but at the youth level, you don't need lactate tests. There you must learn step by step how soccer can be played in a quite specific way: a good technique on the offensive and a lot of creativity in play making!

Authors: *Can the term "freedom" be seen as another magic word in Dutch youth soccer?*

HS: Absolutely! The Netherlands is a country that celebrates freedom, and in our culture one must and has the right to make mistakes, for this is the only way to learn. I have also worked as a PSV youth coach with video analysis, in which we were not only looking for tactical issues but also how individual players present themselves in the technical and mental areas. We then planned training sessions based on these findings.

And in these sessions, the players had to play with complete freedom, and again make mistakes. The coach corrected them and the players again had to work on their mistakes. Let the children pass, dribble, feint and develop a good game intelligence (spelinzicht) with their unfettered freedom. And if they lose the championships by one point, it doesn't matter. *De toekomst is belangrijk – the future is important!*

6.4 Individual Coaching: The Current Playing, Coaching and Training Philosophy of Ajax Amsterdam (Dutch Champions 2011)

When coaching philosophy is discussed in the world of youth soccer, the name Ajax immediately springs to mind. In April 2009, Franz Hoek and Paul van Veen of the Dutch magazine *TrainersMagazine* were able to interview Head Youth Coordinator Jan Olde Riekerink about the development of the Ajax coaching philosophy.

H/van V: *What is the objective of the Ajax youth section?*

OR: To coach each player individually so that they can go onto play for the Ajax team.

H/van V: *Do you need to attain a certain number of players per year?*

OR: No, but 50% of our pro team must come from our own youth section.

H/van V: *Is this target achievable at the moment?*

OR: Yes, it is. But the question is whether one can measure this. After all, we have seven players we have trained ourselves, but then we don't win the Champions League. So what is the value of this objective then? The most important objective of club must be for the pro team to play internationally at the highest level. That is the Champions League. That is the criterion and the ambition with which players are coached at Ajax.

H/van V: *What is the outlook for the next 10 years?*

OR: That is hard to say. We have many talented players, and we can say that they are really talented. But we can never say where the greatest talent lies. We have to anticipate that for future developments.

H/van V: *What is the Vision for the youth section to be able to achieve this objective?*

OR: We must ask, what exactly does Vision mean? I recently had a discussion about the time when Wesley Sneijder, Rafael van der Vaart, Nigel de Jong, John Heitinga and Urby Emanuelson were playing in the youths, and I myself was a youth coach. We were still training on a rough, old artificial pitch. But they all became top players. Today, we try to improve the conditions in order to coach the players as pros. This happens with the help of a player database, better pitches, more computers, more frequent chats and video analyses, etc. But before, we had none of this and yet we were still able to produce top players. Times have changed but we should not forget that it is all about the game of soccer.

H/van V: *What has changed?*

OR: One simple thing is the lack of exercise these days. We try to compensate for this with the training of multi-skills, such as judo and gymnastics. We are pioneers in terms of gymnastics teaching. We are doing it in conjunction with primary schools. We are now trying to offer this training in clubs by specialist teachers.

H/van V: *What results have you had with multi-skills?*

OR: It is hard to measure, as one must be very honest. We are convinced that multi-skills are effective. Yoga and similar activities are also very interesting for increasing flexibility. We discuss these things for our coaching.

H/van V: *What does the weekly training plan for Ajax youth look like?*

OR: The oldest age group trains 6 times and the youngest 3 times per week. You must make this distinction in the coaching because from U9 to U12, the children come to the club with their parents. Then we have set up a system where they are collected from school and brought to Ajax by minibus. Once at Ajax, they do three things: homework, eat and train. Then they are taken home by minibus. In this stage in their lives, they get a **rounded education.**

H/van V: *Do they play in fixed playing formations?*

OR: The very youngest play 1-3-1-3, then 1-3-4-3, and from the U13 onward, we play 1-4-3-3, with the option in mind to play 1-3-4-3 again. With the youngest, the formation is not so important, as the focus is more on individual development. I think that one should play in three lines. Actually, 1-3-2-3 is even better because players have more space. But still, individual coaching is more important than the formation. That is why we play 1-3-4-3, because it allows better pitch coverage and is the most logical system for playing together. Defensively, it is easy to organize because many players get into a 1 on 1 situation and are not so reliant on team tactics, but on individual tactical contributions. Then comes an age group in which tactics become more and more important. Then you must choose: who is stronger, our opponents or us? Do we have enough fast strikers or not? When is the best time to start an attack? **In short, you learn to play together.**

H/van V: *Is how the pros play important?*

OR: Before we talk about playing styles and formations, we should ask an important question: in which natural environment do we let the players play? Whether we let Bryan Roy or Jesper Gronkjaer play on the left wing creates a difference. They are two completely different types of player. One can play 1-4-3-3, but the way you play and with which types of player in which position is determined by the players. In tactics, it is always about the intention, about how one plays. I believe that we must coach players so that they can have choices.

H/van V: *What do you mean by letting players play in their natural environment?*

OR: If you have a goldfish and you have the choice of putting it in a container with gravel or water, anyone would choose water. Now have a discussion about where a player must stand when the formation is taken away. You have an empty pitch, divide it into zones and place the player somewhere on it.

This is how we talk with our technical staff. Place the player where he can function best, irrespective of the formation. A player like Emanuelson plays best as an inside left in midfield. Because he is creative, he can cope well with the space. He must have space in front of him because he is dynamic, he must come up to goal and he can then score. He must have the creativity to be able to dodge to the right or left. If he is defending, he must have a lot of space behind him because another player must fill this space from behind. In this way, we place the players in a pigeonhole, and when there are three players in one pigeonhole, then we start to push. This is how everyone can get into the best position for them. Eventually, in this way, we try to put our best team together. We can also change our minds, but if we talk about players in this way, then we are really talking about individuals, developments and the player's talents. What can he do and what can't he do?

H/van V: *Does it require talent to spot where individual players can play best in the context of the team development process?*

OR: Yes, it does take talent, and a lot of experience. Experience helps you pick out and simplify little things from a big, complex whole. The same is true for driving a car: when you are a learner, you are just concerned with the technical things in the car; later, you must also look out for traffic. If you drive badly at first, then you wonder how you will manage to cope with everything, but when you have experience, you can drive quite normally. You have more time and space to observe things.

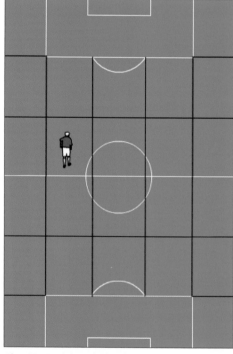

Fig. 13: Positional play in zones.

H/van V: *Are players already allocated a specific position at the start of their training?*

OR: I think that this time comes from U13 and U14 onward. But even then they don't play in a specific position, as we think it is a good idea to let players play in different positions. This week, a player found it hard mentally playing in a certain position, so the coach decided to let him play another week in a worse position. Mental ability can be as decisive as soccer-technical ability. Players must do their best, irrespective of which position they are playing in. But you can't say when you are losing 2:0, now we will do our best because now we want to win. **You must always do your best. I have never coached winning, but always the process. That is the key for the players.** At Ajax, I introduced the idea of the coach filling in a form with instructions for the team and for the individual players. The coach is responsible for the debriefing. They don't need to use a grading system, although I have done it because grading is clearest.

H/van V: *When you have chosen a specific position for a player, does he specialize in it?*

OR: In the youngest age groups, we let the children play freely, and when they turn 15, we try to develop position-specific qualities. One of our emphases is individual development and so we have also specialized the coaching staff. So we have, an individual technique coach, an individual running coach and an individual mental coach. There is still a lot of room to develop players into other positions. Michael Reizinger started off as a right-winger and ended up as a right outside back. However, I think there is a big difference between midfield defenders and wing backs. Many coaches also put a right outside back in the center, although it is a fundamentally different position. A right outside back is more similar to a midfield player as he must anticipate covering tasks forward, therefore both should be good at covering space and

quickly push into the width. A midfield defender though must only push sideways. They are often players who can only think one-dimensionally.

H/van V: *Do you use a curriculum at Ajax?*

OR: I have two different curricula. The first is a general one, which is used for every player whether he is 8 or 35. We are currently writing a specific curriculum, but it is important that it will be implemented. Toon Hermans (late Dutch comedian) once said, "I have written a long letter, as I don't have time to write a short one." We in the Netherlands are champions at writing long curricula, which are never put into practice. In soccer, many curricula are not effective. If you set 100 criteria for what must be done in E juniors, then you can no longer see the forest for the trees because you then have to name and describe so many things. You must not only write them but monitor them. But what do you often see? We put many things into a curriculum and do not monitor them, as happens, for example, with set pieces. Here, many things can be noticed. If in a defensive corner, I see a player relaxing at the long post, then I get angry. Somewhere in his education he must learn to play correctly, and something like that belongs in a curriculum.

H/van V: *Where is it decided whether a player stays at Ajax or leaves?*

OR: That is basic knowledge or instinct; it's decided by four or five people. And let's be honest, anyone can choose the four best and the four worst. In between those extremes, there are always nuances and differences of opinion. You have to actually watch the player who is not yet physically mature. You must be patient. It is not just about keeping the best players but the players with the most talent. As the most importance nuance, we also take their date of birth into account.

H/van V: *Do you also look at positions?*

OR: No, we look at talent. The only problem is that talent can be spotted, but you never know how far it can be developed. The quality of the coach in the coaching process is very important. The coach must provide the player with optimal pedagogical and soccer-specific guidance. They must know the general facts about soccer, but also the specific issues that relate to the age group they work with. I think they must assess players both according to their strengths and weaknesses. The players with the most talent work separately on their weaknesses alongside the team training. We do this from U15 onward. This can also include running technique, which I personally consider to be important. It's not that we want to coach track athletes, but running plays an important role in soccer.

H/van V: *What do you think is important in a good coach?*

OR: Generally, the most important thing is that they have the same vision. The ideal coach does not exist; every coach is different and that's a good thing, so that each one shows his specific qualities and can transfer these qualities to the players. **However, he must absolutely know the basic principles of coaching and that coaching is more important than winning.** In addition, in his coaching work, he must be able to work in a very detailed way.

H/van V: *You say that in soccer, there are different facts. Can you give an example of this?*

OR: Two basic starting points are important: the ball is in movement and the players are in movement. That may sound simple, but if you think about it more carefully, you come to an analysis in soccer. It is all about in which direction the ball is kicked, dribbled or moved. Players must be able to recognize that.

H/van V: *How do you see the position of Ajax Amsterdam in the Netherlands?*

OR: We have a clear philosophy. We have a clear strategy with which to implement this philosophy and the club has a special past. In addition, we employ many people. History has made us what we are today.

6.5   Be Dominant and Create Positional Play: The Current Coaching and Training Philosophy of FC Twente Enschede
(Dutch Champions 2010)

Last year in particular, the Dutch national league club Twente Enschede attracted national and international attention when the seniors won the Dutch championships (2009/2010) and will play for the Netherlands in the Champions League. On Jan. 12, 2010, the authors were able to conduct an in-depth interview with professional soccer coach (coach betaald voetbal), head youth coach and U23 coach René Hake in Enschede about the coaching and training philosophy of FC Twente Enschede. Since about 20% of youth players at the club are German citizens, it was interesting to learn to what extent they influence the club's coaching and training philosophy.

Authors: *What is Twente Enschede's coaching and training philosophy?*

RH: Every morning we get to the club around 8:30am. Then the pro and U23 coaching staff sort out the training programs for the players and teams. For the U23s, we also prepare individual training and group chats. From 10am to noon, we train, then lunch is from 12:30pm to 1pm. After lunch, the coaching staff prepares the afternoon workouts. Again we prepare the training in smaller groups. Then the next training session takes place from 2:30pm to 4:30pm. After the session, there are individual chats that usually last until 6pm. Depending on what else is planned, we then usually scout more players.

Authors: *How is the collaboration with the pro section structured?*

RH: The collaboration with the pros is very good. We discuss players, planning and training content.

Authors: *Please describe your objectives in the children's, youth and U23 areas*

RH: The coaching objectives are set for every age group:

- U12 and U13: **Basic playing ability** to match playing ability.

- U14: Use the game as a way to achieve match playing ability. Play more soccer without the ball than with the ball. That means: play **more with the head** than with the legs.

- U15: **Match playing ability** (11v11). The players should implement game situations that arise in different formations and are therefore explainable. The players should also learn to develop specific actions in different game situations.

- U16: **Championship ability.** The players should learn to develop different actions and be able to relate them to the team function. They should recognize game situations and act purposefully. In addition, each player's special qualities (talents) should be developed. The question of "who is suited to which position?" should start to be explored in training.

- U17: **Championship ability.** The U16 objectives are still relevant, but players should now learn to work with **different formations** (their own and the opposing team's). The players must learn to deal with different consequences.

- U19: Coaching of optimal ability, aiming for **top class soccer.** Learning how to win a match. 1) Training in playing position. 2) Becoming a specialist and learning what is required in different tasks. 3) Learning to do one's utmost for team success.

- U23: This is the **"sub team"** of the professional side. It therefore possesses an identical playing approach, organization and way of playing. It is the final stage of coaching. At the national level, the team plays in the U23 Championships (*Beloftencompetitie*) of the KNVB. It should always be the aim of the U23s to finish below the first five teams.

Other targets are:

1. To prepare the players gradually and with many individual training sessions for professional level.

2. To work on the mental area: what am I prepared to do to be successful (intrinsic motivation)?

Authors: *What do you look for first when recruiting a coach (license or knowledge)?*

RH: What the coach knows and does is the most important thing. We also need coaches to have a certain license and give the coaches the possibility of attending certain advanced courses so that they can keep improving.

Authors: *You work at Twente Enschede near the German border. How many German youth players train and play at Twente and is there a difference between German and Dutch youth players?*

RH: In eight different teams from U12 to U23, there are 160 players, of which 29 come from Germany. That is about 20%. There are big differences between German and Dutch players, which can be roughly expressed as the German players being much better trained in regard to the necessary discipline than the Dutch players.

Authors: *What do your coaches look out for in particular in everyday training?*

RH: For us, the players' attitude to their own performance is important (intrinsic motivation). Of course, the emphases in the different age groups are structured differently (c.f. the above mentioned age-groups).

Authors: *What is the typical team management like at Twente Enschede?*

RH: At FC Twente we have certain rules relating to how we treat each other. Examples of this are: the coach is addressed as "coach", no caps should be worn indoors and in the changing rooms, no cell phones should be used. In addition, all age groups up to U16 should play with black soccer boots. Between U16 and U19, players may also wear boots in FC Twente colors. From U19 onwards, players may choose the color of their boots. They must also tuck their shirt into their shorts on the pitch and their socks must never be pulled up above their knees.

Authors: *How is the coaching structured at FC Twente?*

RH: The coaching is primarily determined by the playing process. It is geared both to the team and to individual players. Players must be developed by ongoing coaching, which should also lead to an improvement in results. Here too there is a constant differentiation: the older the player, the more important the results.

Authors: *You often play friendly matches against German youth teams. What do you find particularly noticeable in these encounters?*

RH: When we play German teams, I find that they often use counter-attacks. They often stand in blocks together, which even include the strikers. This makes the spaces compact and narrow. They can play like this for 90 minutes. The willingness of each player to place himself at the service of the team is fantastic. When they gain possession of the ball, they quickly play deep and try to pass to the strikers who are often good at finding space. When they have the ball they often try to play from behind. The discipline of the Germans is unique and it often gives rise to interesting matches. That is why we try to arrange up to eight friendly matches a year against German clubs for all our teams.

7 Dutch Technique Coaching in Theory and Practice

> "I admit that I'm not particularly interested in scoring ugly goals."
> (Dennis Bergkamp; quoted in Winner, 2008, page 206)

Based on the TIC model, in The Netherlands, the coaching of technical ability and skills is a priority in youth soccer. The basic techniques of dribbling, passing, shooting, heading, receiving and running with the ball as well as various feints are considered to be essential performance components, which can be trained well into the senior ranks. Geurts (1999, page 35) assumes that on the basis of the mastery of these basic techniques other effective elements can be developed such as feeling for the ball, game intelligence, feel for the game and action speed. These elements are seen as decisive for a future high performance level in The Netherlands (ibid). Technique training should be carefully prepared and considered and developed playfully according to the perspective of the Zeist Vision (c.f. Chapter 9.1): a player with good technique can find a solution to a particular match situation more quickly (c.f. te Poel, 1995a, page 102-107; ibid, 1995b, pages 122-128).

7.1 Technique Learning

The KNVB does not support the isolated training of technique for children. "Driving a car is best learnt when you sit behind the wheel and join the traffic, and the same is also true for technique training. You must play soccer in order to learn the techniques." (van Amstel, 1.28.2003).

According to the KNVB method of technique(s) learning, the coach should limit the observation of all situations in a game to corrections that concern the control or lack of control of the ball (c.f. van Lingen, 2001, page 88). In addition, the Dutch children's coach should initiate via the setting of so-called motivating homework tasks the ongoing process of "self-coaching and learning" of the basic techniques in the players' free time (c.f. Seeverens, 2001b, page 20; Michels & Vergoossen, 2001).

A training example for the development of soccer techniques in children's soccer in The Netherlands is the stedenspel.

It should be played as follows:

Organization:

- Mark out a 30m x 30m square.
- At each corner of the square, set up another small 5 x 5m square.
- These small squares are named after cities (e.g., Groningen, Maastricht, Amsterdam and The Hague).
- Every player gets a ball.

Procedure

- The players dribble slowly or quickly through the large square (the country).
- They can dribble through the country, carry the ball in their hands, or pass the ball from country to country.
- The coach calls out the name of a city, and the players must take the ball to the corresponding square quickly.
- However, the players can also run across the circle. They may travel from city to city.
- The players can pass the ball away from each other and disturb the others when dribbling (match-typical dribbling training).

Objectives

- Using this game, the players learn to pass, shoot and dribble.
- It trains reaction speed.
- A competitive element is produced: which player is quickest to Amsterdam?
- The coach can encourage the youngsters with child-appropriate language in order to improve their technique: "who can swim fastest to The Hague?"

The cities game is an excellent representation of the KNVB vision with regard to the development of technique in Dutch children's soccer (see van Lingen, 2001, pps 92-95).

7.2 Youth Technique Training Using Example Passing Drills With or Without Shots on Goal

Junior level starts from C juniors onward in the Netherlands. The demands on the players should now be focused on *team play* (see KNVB, 1996, p 43). *Game intelligence* and *communication* from the TIC model are considered essential priorities in the training process (see Chapter 4.2.1). The technique should be further refined in everyday training with game and exercise forms. Training drills that practice these basic demands for technique training in junior soccer are called *passing forms with shot on goal* (*afwerkvormen) and passing forms (trapvormen)* and can be found below.

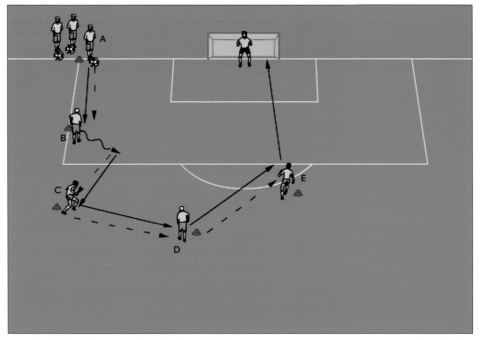

Fig. 14: Stop-combination with shot on goal

Procedure

- One player stands at each of the five cones placed in front of a goal with goalkeeper.

- Player A starts the action with a pass to B and runs after his pass; B quickly stops the ball and passes it to player C.

- Player C passes the ball back to D, who "pokes" the ball forward to E who then shoots on goal.

Coaching

- Every player starts from a lunge position.

- Every player performs a preliminary action (*vooractie*) before playing the ball.

- "Run toward" slow balls.

Variations

- Only play with a certain foot.

- Shoot on goal within a certain time (time pressure).

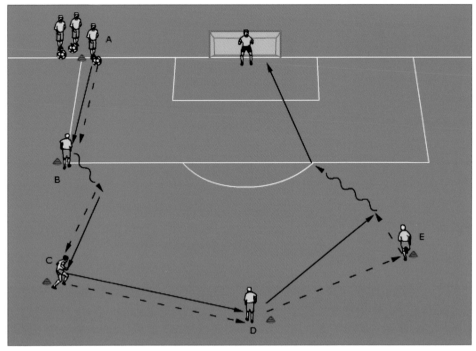

Fig. 15: Volley combination with shot on goal

Procedure

- As in Fig. 14 with larger gaps between the cones.

- Only volley passes are allowed.

- Player D lobs the last ball to player E, who then shoots on goal with a volley or drop kick.

Coaching

- "Fast" volleys, no free-kick training.

- Fast ball control, taking the ball to the side.

Variations

- Perform all elements with opponents (opponent pressure).

- Additional 1 on 1 before the shot on goal.

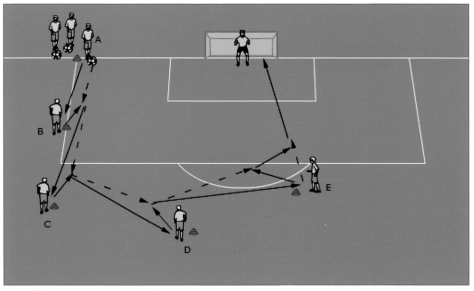

Fig. 16: Rebounds (kaatsvormen)

Procedure

- Set up as in Fig. 14.

- Every player lets the ball "rebound" and takes over the other's position, thus giving rise to a sort of circuit.

- At the end of the passing sequence, player E shoots on goal.

- The new action is started again from position A.

Coaching

- Hard and accurate passing.

- Little ball rotation.

- The toes of the standing leg point forward.

- Keep the eyes on the ball when changing positions after letting the ball rebound.

Variations

- Only pass the ball with a certain foot.

- Only when the command "rebound" is given can play continue.

- Perform all tasks with opponents.

Fig. 16: Rebound game with volleys

Procedure

- As in Fig. 16, but the balls now must be passed as volleys.

- The last ball from player D to E is passed as a running lob, so that player E shoots on goal with a volley or dropkick.

Coaching

- Don't step into the ball.

- Pass the ball with the outside of the foot sometimes (surprise effect).

- Keep your eyes on the ball when passing it.

Variations

- Only let the ball rebound off the head.

- Only let the ball rebound off the foot.

- Only let the ball rebound off a specific foot.

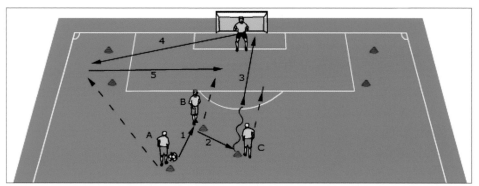

Fig. 18: Pass to a third player, then cross

Procedure

- Three players play about 25m in front of a wide goal with goalkeeper.

- Three groups carry out the drill one after the other (slightly to the right/slightly to the left/centrally).

- Player A passes the ball to B, who lets it rebound to C, who dribbles it and shoots on goal.

- During this time, player A runs to the outside, where a cone goal has been placed almost perpendicular to the end line.

- The goalkeeper receives the ball from C and quickly throws the ball (aim: fast game opening) through the cone goal.

- Player takes the ball and crosses it to players B and C who are running into the center, ready to shoot on goal.

Coaching

- Pass hard and fast between the three players.

- The players' positions should always be slightly staggered and start with a preliminary action!

- Don't shoot at the keeper's legs but slightly to the side.

Variations

- Competition: goalkeeper against field players. Who scores the most goals?

- The goalkeeper must play a dropkick into a cone goal!

- On the wings, another 1v1 is played (cross after opponent pressure).

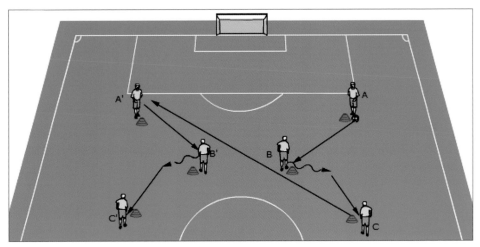

Fig. 19: Long passing from a 1-4-3-3 formation

Procedure

- Place 6 cones on a pitch measuring about 25m x 20m.

- Player A passes to player B; player B performs a preliminary action, turns and passes to player C.

- Player C performs a preliminary action, takes the ball, turns and passes to A1 on the other side.

- After every action, the players run to their new positions.

- Players B and B1 represent positions 6 and 8 in the 1-4-3-3 system. These players pass inward and must turn outward.

Coaching

- When passing the ball inward and when turning outward, ensure the "correct" foot is used.

- The rebound must be played accurately and sensitively.

- Include preliminary actions and anticipate where the ball will be passed.

- Mutual coaching and verbal encouragement: where should the ball be passed?

Variations

- Pass after one ball contact.

- Two ball touches are mandatory.

- Dribble every time you receive the ball.

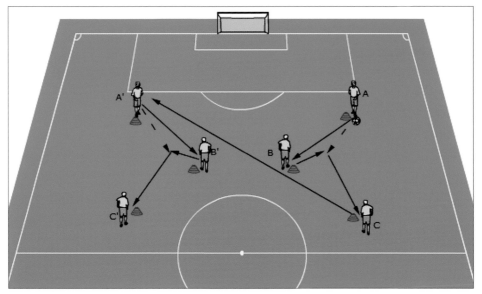

Fig. 20: Long passing from a 1-4-3-3 formation (part 2)

Procedure

- See Fig. 19

- Player A passes to B, who lets the ball bounce back to player A. A passes to C, who passes the ball to A1.

- After every action, the players run to the next position.

- Change direction: clockwise and counter-clockwise.

- Increase the gaps and possibly play with two balls.

- Players B and B1 represent positions 6 and 8 in a 1-4-3-3 formation. These pass inward and must turn outward.

Coaching

- Pass back with the "wrong" foot.

- Coach the rebounding from the player who passes the ball.

- Precise and hard passing game.

Variations

- Player A passes the ball to C, who again lets the ball rebound back to A. Then repeat with player B. Player A passes to C, who lets the ball rebound to the now free player B. B lets the ball rebound back to C who passes the ball to A.

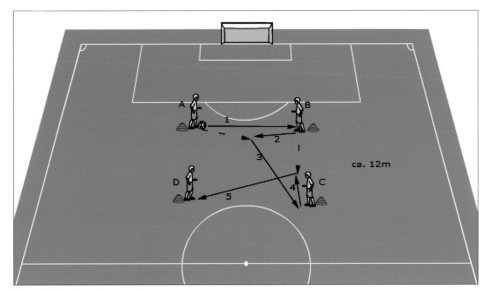

Fig. 21: Passing in a square

Procedure

- Place cones 12m apart at the corners of a square.

- Player A passes the ball to B, B lets it rebound forward, A runs toward the ball and passes it diagonally to C, who lets the ball rebound forward to B who runs toward it, etc.

- Each player runs to the next cone.

Coaching

- The players start from a preliminary movement, never from a standstill.

- Don't spin the ball when letting it rebound.

- Always keep your eyes on the ball and run the shortest distance to the next cone.

Variations

- All tasks have two mandatory ball touches (for ball reception and running with the ball).

- Competition: two passing squares side by side. Which square is faster?

- Add a shot on goal.

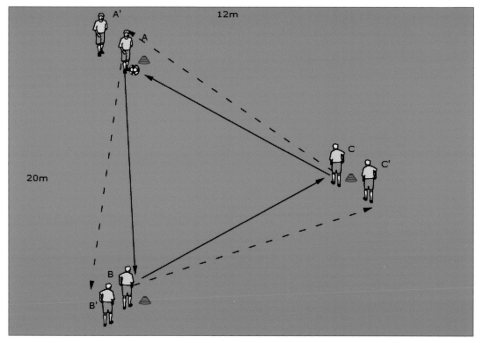

Fig. 22: Long passing in a triangle with six players

Procedure

- Six players play on a 20m x 12m pitch.

- Only play direct passes with change of position.

- After passing the ball, the players stand behind the next player.

Coaching

- Precise and hard passing game.

- Keep the eyes on the ball after passing it.

- Pass with the inside of the foot.

- Remember to pass with both feet.

Variations

- Only pass with the right foot.

- Only pass with the left foot.

- Play the first pass as a volley.

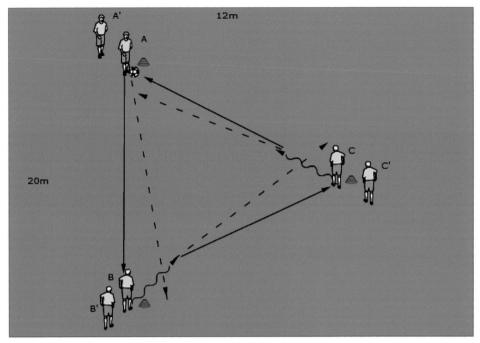

Fig. 23: Long passing in a triangle with 6 players (part 2)

Procedure

- See Fig. 22, but with the first pass, player B controls the ball and dribbles while performing feints.

- Player A now puts him under pressure and B must execute "realistic" feints and then pass the ball to player C.

Coaching

- The first pass is passed hard.

- The first touch from B "sticks" to the foot.

- The defensive player adopts a lunge position when playing 1 on 1.

Variations

- A cone goal is placed in the middle of the triangle and players play 1 on 1 through the cone goal.

- The first ball is passed by a lob.

- Player B first takes the ball to the side and then plays 1 on 1 against player A.

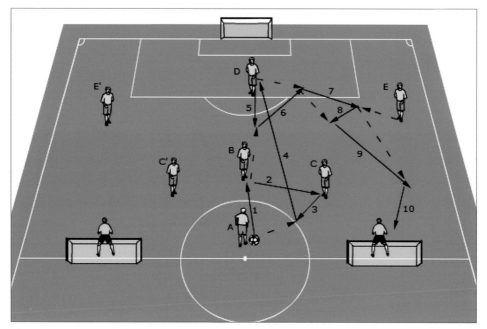

Fig. 24: Passing with the "10-combination"

Procedure

- The players play into two goals (side by side) with goalkeepers on half a pitch. The ball should be passed around to the right and/or left.

- Player A passes to B, who lets the ball rebound. C lets the ball rebound to incoming player A. A passes a long ball to D, who lets the ball rebound to B, who then plays a one-two back to D. D passes the ball to E, who plays a one-two back to D. D plays the "killer" pass to E and E completes the combination and moves into position A. Each player moves around one position.

Coaching

- Always perform with preliminary actions.

- Ask for fast ball speed.

- Keep watching the ball.

Variations

- Reduce the gaps between the players (slower ball speed).

- Increase the gaps between the players (faster ball speed).

- Competition: who shoots fastest into one of the two goals?

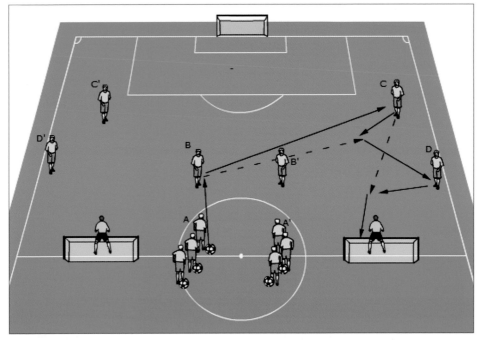

Fig. 25: Passing in group of six

Procedure

- See Fig. 24, but the passing should be faster.

- Player A passes the ball to B, who turns and plays a long, flat pass to C. C returns the ball to the incoming B1. B1 passes to D, and he lets the ball rebound into the path of player C. C completes the move with a shot on goal.

- Sequence starts at position A and A1, and each player moves around one position.

Coaching

- Pass the ball to the "correct" foot.

- The players coach each other.

- Don't spin the ball when it rebounds.

Variations

- Two ball touches are mandatory.

- Only play the pass after dribbling and then stopping the ball.

- Throw in a few feints when dribbling.

Players' technical abilities and skills undergo a position-specific improvement as a result of using the above forms and are typical of Dutch technique training. That means that in the junior age groups, a functional technique should be aimed for that corresponds to the tasks of each position within the team (see Seeverens, 2001b, p 20). So, for example, the left back plays on the left in training games and should focus on position-specific technical abilities and skills when crossing under pressure and dribbling with the left foot, for instance (see Kormelink & Seeverens, 1999b, p 71; see also Chapter 8.4).

7.3 From the Coerver Method to Coerver® Coaching

In Dutch youth soccer, the now internationally renowned and recognized *Coerver Method* has a completely different approach to Zeist Vision. The famous "brand name" of *Coerver® Coaching* uses the *Coerver Method*, which was developed especially for children and young players by the Dutch soccer coach Wiel Coerver in the 1970s. When he started to develop his method, Coerver believed that youth players should develop different techniques mainly using isolated drills (technique-oriented ball training). The influence of the opponent is less important in *Coerver Method* drills. "Soccer is only easy for the few top players who can outsmart opponents with their technical skills and their speed into a small space and under pressure" (Coerver, March 17, 2003). The development of feeling for the ball is the main coaching emphasis of the *Coerver Method*. According to Galustian and Cooke (1998, p 7), individual players learn their technique through countless repetitions, without the need to replicate a match situation. Through the permanent repetition of a target technique (e.g., the Rivelino Trick)[14], the players should automatize the trick to such an extent that they can also master this specific technique in a match against an opponent. "The specific sequence of a specific technique is deliberately trained" (Kormelink & Seeverens, 1998a, p 21), so that the coach in the *Coerver® Coaching* system must fulfill certain demands: "the young player must be trained by the coach who can perfectly demonstrate all feints and other ball techniques by Pelé, Cruyff, Maradonna, Romario, van Basten, etc." (Coerver, March 17, 2003). Individual techniques are therefore the hallmark of the Coerver Method, which a child or young player can practice alone or in a group. *Coerver® Coaching* assumes that Players initially improve their skills individually before being able to evolve further in a second step in the group and team process (see Galustin & Cooke, 1998). This puts the (explicit) *Coerver Method*, with its multitude of exercise forms from the '70s and '80s, at odds with the implicit learning and teaching method of the KNVB.

---

14 Named after the eponymous Brazilian player and also known as the Elastico. The trick is performed as follows: start by dribbling at medium speed, then facing an opponent, flick the ball up to one side. In mid-air, cushion the ball with the inside of your foot, taking it the other way past your marker.

However, an analysis of Coerver's recent publications, which are supported worldwide by Alfred Galustin, Charlie Cooke and John Collins as "co-founders of Coerver® Coaching" from 2005 (*Make your Move*), 2008 (*Improve your Game*), and 2010 (*Coerver® Coaching: Über individuelle Klasse zum Erfolg*) the *Coerver Method* curriculum has been extended in the following areas:

- **"1 on 1"** to goals or objects.
- **"Soccer Moves"**: current feints as performed in world soccer that should be used and practiced in specific situations and with specific intentions.
- **"Skills"** and **"Super Skills"**: Coerver moves to improve footwork, flexibility and coordination.
- **"Strength"**: soccer-specific elements of the core skills strength, endurance and speed that should be trained specifically.
- **"Science"**: acquisition and implementation of current sports science knowledge to optimize youth soccer performance.

Coerver and his "co-founders" show with these new publications that they have broadened the originally purely technique-oriented approach to include tasks. "Instead of "learning from feinting," the target is instead the "effective implementation of what has been learned" (Galustin & Wieczorek, 2010, p 31). So although they now partly follow current sports science findings in ball game research, they still leave many questions unanswered in the *Coerver® Coaching* method levels for the coaching of playing techniques according to the "Three Step Program" and the triad "learn, consolidate and implement" (Galustian & Wieczorek, 2010, p 33):

- How long should the phase of "pure" technique repetition be?
- Is it more effective to include perceptive and tactical demands in training directly after the first technique practice?
- Coaching of technique is determined by the demands of the game, which also requires great technical variability. Should technique variability be performed according to set or random guidelines (see Hohmann, Kölb & Roth, 2005; Mechling & Munzert, 2003)?

The Dutchman Wiel Coerver inspired youth soccer coaching throughout the world with his original Coerver drills, from which many soccer coaches went on to develop other "feints" and coaching systems that aim to optimize players' creativity (see Chapter 7.4).

Even though the Zeist Vision of the KNVB considers the technical coaching of young players from a different didactic and methodological perspective, many Dutch youth coaches do work with the *Coerver Method* and *Coerver® Coaching*.

Kormelink and Seeverens (1998a, p 21) state that "the basic techniques are fundamental prerequisites for the soccer player and therefore players must practice by themselves with the ball every day from the age of 6."

The Coerver Method is the starting point for the following "methods" (see Chapter 7.4) and the Van Dijk Method (*Soccer Training. Techniques and Exercises, www.vandijkmethod.com*). The Dutchman Van Dijk tries to bridge the gap between grassroots and high performance soccer with his method of coaching individual technical abilities and skills in youth soccer.

Figure 26 shows the six building blocks of the *Coerver® Coaching* **Program**, which every trained "Coerver Coach" should use as a guideline for the coaching stages. The structure of the pyramid reflects the dominance and great importance of "ball mastery," and ball receiving and passing in Coerver's method.

Fig. 26: The Coerver Pyramid (after Galustian & Cook, 1998, p 7)

Legend
- Group Attack (decisive fast attacking)
- Finishing (commitment to shooting on goal)
- Speed (speed and dynamism with or without the ball)
- Moves (1 on 1) (learning to solve 1-on-1 situations creatively and successfully with a diverse range of movement forms)
- Receiving & Passing ("1st touch," brave and creative passing)
- Ball Mastery (with both feet)

Below are practical examples for each layer of the Coerver Pyramid.

First Layer: Ball Mastery

Fig. 27: Skill "Pull Through Turn"

Procedure

1. Dribble.

2. Raise the left foot and bring it over the ball.

3. Kick the ball lightly back with the left heel.

4. Pass the ball forward in the direction of play with the inside of the right foot.

5. Resume dribbling (see Galustian & Cooke, 2008a).

Fig. 28: Skill "Pull Spin"

Procedure

1. Dribble

2. Place the ball of the right foot on top of the ball.

3. Push down on the ball and change feet so that the ball of the left foot is now on top of the ball.

4. Cushion the pushing and turning movement with the ball of the right foot and the left foot on the ball – possibly turning further and change of passing direction (see Galustian & Cooke, 2008a).

Procedure

Throw-in to volley and half-volley with three intermediate steps.

Variations

- Inside of the boot-outside of the boot-instep-thigh-chest-head.
- Change passing length and height.
- Use different ball rotations.
- Use balls of different sizes (see Galustian & Cooke, 2008b).

Equipment variations

See above.

Fig. 29: Ball Mastery in Groups of Three

Fig. 30: Tchoukball,
rebound frame in threes

Fig. 31: Wall rebound in threes

Second Layer: Receiving and Passing in Threes

Fig. 32:
Receiving and
passing in threes

Procedure
- Straight passing.
- Ball reception with the outside of the foot (first touch).
- Reception with the inside front of the foot .
- Straight return pass (second touch).
- Change sides.

Coaching
Make sure players use both feet.

Variations
- Reception with the inside of the boot and return pass with the same foot or vice versa (rhythm: outside of the foot – inside of the foot, or vice versa)
- Diagonal return pass.
- Diagonal return lob from the ankle.
- Reception behind the support leg.
- Throw-in.
  - Reception with the chest.
  - Return pass with the inside and outside of the foot.
  - Reception with the thigh, return pass with the inside and outside of the foot.
  - Reception with the inside and outside of the foot and headed return pass.
  - Reception with the head and headed return pass (see Galustian & Cooke, 2008b).

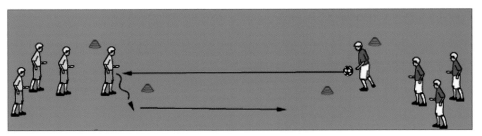

Fig. 33: Receiving and Passing (eight players)

Procedure

Straight, flat pass and reception (first touch) and straight return pass (second touch).

Set-up

• Two cone triangles facing each other (length of the sides depends on players' ability).
• Distance between the triangles should be between 10-15m.

Variations

• Reception with the right foot, return pass with the right foot.
• Reception with the left foot, return pass with the right foot.
• Change of direction.
• Lob with reception.
• Instep kicks with reception.
• Kicks with the outside of the foot with reception.
• With four triangles and diagonal and straight return passes (see Galustian & Cooke, 2008b).

Third Layer: Moves 1 on 1

Procedure

• "1 on 1 frontal"
  • Sprint past the opponent with explosive acceleration and with the ball.
• Possibilities
  • Attacker feints between two cones to the left and right and then decides to dribble fast to the left or right.
  • The player without the ball sprints afterhim.
• Who can run through the cone goal (6-10m away, left and right) first?
• Whole form: triangle.

Fig. 34: 1 on 1 Speed Drill (Full Pressure)

Variations

• Feint without a ball.
• Feint with a stationary ball (see Galustian & Cooke, 2005).

Fourth Layer: Speed

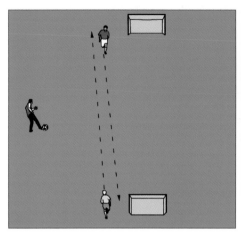 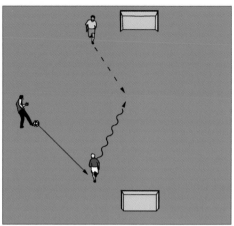

Fig. 35a and 35b: Speed Drill

Procedure

- 1-on-1 frontal into two mini goals
  - Sprint, stop and turn, sprint and pass to the fastest player (reward) by the late rally-positioned coach.
  - Ball reception at highest speed.
  - 1 on 1 with shot on goal.

Variations

- Two adjoining pitches, four mini goals and two coaches: goals may also be scored on the adjoining pitch (variability pressure).
- Both sides compete at the same time (complexity pressure).
- With four or six players and a lateral pass (2v2 into 4 goals).
- Exchange the mini goals for wide goals plus goalkeepers.
- Vary the playing direction (forward, backward) and speed, spin variations, height variations.
- Change the pitch size and shape (triangle, rectangle, square, lozenge, circle) (see Galustian & Cooke, 2005).

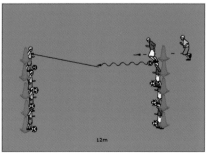

12m

Procedure

- 1 on 1 with opponent from the side-rear.
- Fast dribbling with opponent pressure.
- Shot on goal toward the cones.
- The next player then follows, dribbling fast.

Fig. 36: Speed and concentration under great pressure (1 on 1 in group)

Variation

- Team competition: who is first in the team to kick all the cones?
- Pitch size: 10m x 10m.
- Establish the sequence of the fast dribbling (see Galustian & Cooke, 2005).

Fifth Layer: **Finishing**

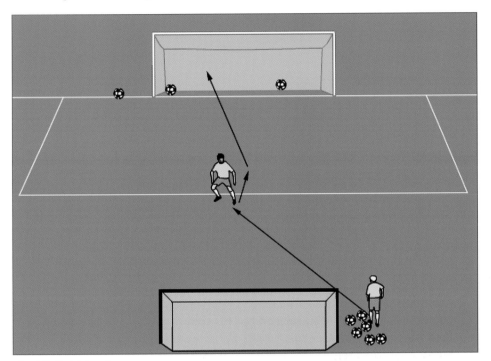

Fig. 37: Finishing One

Procedure

- In groups of two or three with two wide goals.
- Reception with back to the empty goal.
- "Chip" the ball.
- Turn and volley shot on goal with the instep.
- Change goals when all the balls are in the net.

Variations

Bilateral play: different passing directions; different passing types; with goalkeepers (see Coerver, no year).

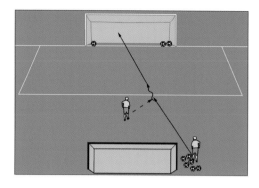

Fig. 38: Finishing Two

Procedure
- See Fig. 37.
- Pass on the run and reception on curved running path (left and right feet)
- Drect shot on goal.

Variations
- See Fig. 37.
- In 1 on 1 and with crosses from right and left.
- Shot on goal through the center (scissors kick, side volley kick, hip turn kick, header).

Other Variations
- With two goalkeepers.
- With central defenders.
- With wing backs (see Coerver, no year).

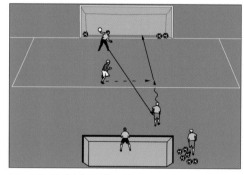

Fig. 39: Finishing Three

Procedure
- See Fig. 38.
- In group of three plus two goalkeepers.
- Goal kick or throw, ball reception with back to own goal
- Dribble
- 1 on 1 (opponent frontal) and direct shot on goal.
- Pitch size dependent upon ability.

Variations
- 1 on 1 with opponent behind.
- Same with 1 on 1 across the half positions (and opponent frontal, behind or at the side).
- Same with 1 on 1 across the wing position.
- Ensure two-footed play.
- Create uneven-sided situations (see Coerver Fundamentals, no year).

Sixth Layer: Group Attack

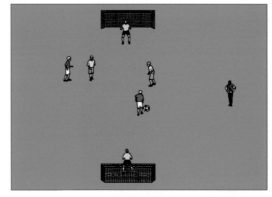

*Fig. 40: Group Attack
2v2 plus two goalkeepers.*

Procedure

- Training games in Figures 40-42.
- From 2v2 into two goals plus goalkeeper to 4v4 into four goals plus goalkeeper to 5v5 into four goals plus goalkeeper.

Coaching

- Frequent goal shooting (rebounds [see Chapter 8.4.3] and volleys; fast dribbling).
  Challenge players to build up attacks and shift the game.
- Make sure players practice with both feet.

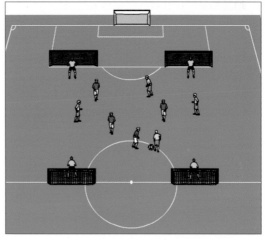

Fig. 41: Group Attack 4v4 plus four goalkeepers

Variations

- Pitch size.
- Additional mini goals on the side lines (game shifting).
- Mark out spaces in color; create uneven-sided situations.
- Change spatial layout (e.g., in Fig. 41, 2v2 or 3v1 instead of diamond-shaped) (see Coerver & Galustian, 1995, p 184-185).

*Fig. 42: Group Attack
5v5 plus four goalkeepers*

7.3.1 Technique, Speed and Self-Confidence: The Sparta Rotterdam Soccer Academy

As can be gathered from the sample training schedules and contents of the children and youth conception of the Sparta Rotterdam[15] soccer academy, the *Coerver Method* and *Coerver® Coaching* are also explicitly practiced in the Dutch national league club. The soccer academy of Sparta Rotterdam was founded with the aim of using committed soccer coaches to work on technical abilities and skills exclusively with isolated training. From the F to A juniors, as well as their own team training, every youth player gets one special weekly *Coerver Method* training session per week (see Voetbalacademie, May 3, 2003).

"In a normal team training session, there is little time to devote to individual technique, which is why we want the kids and young players to learn the tricks and feints perfectly in small groups" (van Lingen, Feb. 23, 2003). "Tactical aspects belong in club training, but here, once a week, the focus is on the practice and repetition of feints, dummies and ball techniques" (McDonald, Feb. 23, 2003).

The soccer academy's youth coaching focuses on about 150 different movements (with or without opponent), which are key elements of the three factors: technique, speed and self-confidence (see Voetbalacademie, May 3, 2003). In the children's and youth conception, we consider that the precise and expert mastery of the main performance components *technique* and *speed* increase enjoyment and enthusiasm, which again make a significant contribution to *self-confidence* (see Voetbal Academie Sparta Rotterdam, 2002, p 2).

The children and juniors of the soccer academy are also given extra written and individually tailored technique training tasks by their coaches that they must practice in their own time (see ibid, p 1).

Even though individual technique training has no place in the curriculum of the KNVB, van Lingen and McDonald report positive effects and experiences in the use and implementation of the *Coerver Method*.

---

15   Sparta Rotterdam was founded in 1888 and currently plays in the second Dutch league (*eerste divisie*). Sparta was 6 times champion (1909, 1911, 1912, 1913 and 1959). In addition, Sparta was 3 times Dutch cup winner (1958, 1962 and 1966).

7.4 Soccer Technique: The René Meulensteen Method and *sportpartners*

René Meulensteen,
Born on March 25, 1964
Dutch and
Current First Team Coach
at internationally renowned soccer club
Manchester United.

At the start of his coaching career, René Meulensteen was youth coach at NEC Nijmegen, technique coach at the Qatar soccer association and head coach at Bröndby Copenhagen. René Meulensteen is a pupil of Wiel Coerver and, alongside his activity at Manchester United in cooperation with Fons van der Brande (the firm Sportpartners – www.sportpartners.nl) the "René Meulensteen Academy," which particularly in the Netherlands (and now also worldwide) offers guided, advanced training in the area of soccer technique. The authors were able to conduct in-depth interviews with René Meulensteen on Feb. 12, 2010 and Fons van den Brande on Feb. 10, 2010 on the significance of technique training in general and the *Coerver Method* in particular in professional soccer.

Interview with René Meulensteen:

Authors: *How do you coach soccer technique?*

RM: That depends upon many things; firstly, on the age group concerned and whether they are juniors or seniors. The ability of the group is also important. **Technique training is repetition!** The coach's job is to make it possible for the players to perform as many repetitions as possible.

This can happen in three ways:

1. Individual training
2. Group training
3. Competitive games, small-sided games and training games

These three types must be coached in such a way that the players are later able to cope in an 11- a side game and can best adjust their technique to their position.

For *children between the ages of 6 and 9*, place the technique on a very broad level, where the learning of movements and the basic techniques of passing, shooting and ball reception should be coached. The coach who works with them must be able to demonstrate and teach these techniques/movements well.

For the *10-12 year-old juniors*, training priorities should above all be speed, creativity and creating match feeling, in order to give players increased self-confidence that they can radiate outward. This also helps them later to develop initiative on the ball. In this age group, the coach must enable the players to further develop the learned techniques by means of fun exercises, match forms and small-sided games.

In the *13-15 age group*, the training focus is primarily the transfer of techniques into an 11-a side match. In my opinion, 11-a side games are played much too early. Why? For many players, the pitch is too big and the game is therefore too tactical and complex for juniors. Young players must slowly grow into playing on a full-size pitch playing 4-a side, 5-a side, 6- a side, 7-a side, 8-a side and 9-a side and be guided gradually into 11-a side games. In these training games, the players must learn and perfect the tactical principles of defense, attack and switching in different zones. These forms also benefit technique training. If the players are 14 or 15 years old, they are capable of understanding situations much better from a tactical point of view, and you will see that they master tactical knowledge in such a way that they have the technical basis to be able to perform things successfully.

René Meulensteen (left)
In conversation with
"the genuine national hero"
(Mail on Sunday; Ferguson, 2000),
Sir Alex Ferguson
(Manager, Manchester United).

At the age of 16-18, the final coaching phase begins, which focuses on the coaching technique with regard to playing 11-a side. The players now develop specifically as defenders, midfield players or forward. The important thing now is that the players are in their positions and specific playing concepts to make the correct decisions within the three above-mentioned types. The players must act with awareness and know that they now can and must implement the techniques they have learned in their offensive game within a match. If players are good and creative, and possess a good balance between the basic techniques and diverse movement around the four 1-on-1 situations *(opponent at your side, opponent in front of you, opponent behind you and diagonally behind you)*, they dominate the game, enable the ball to circulate, can perform one-twos and position changes and are therefore valuable to the team.

In this coaching phase, training work is based around stimulation of awareness, personal responsibility and developing an extreme winning mentality. This group must be presided over by a strong personality who is consistent and can coach with attention to detail with regard to the technique movements in the 11-a side. However, it can often be seen that the coach only wants to win and thereby inhibits or restricts his players from taking different risks. The better a technique has been developed when players are young, the lower the risk of them not being able to cope in an 11-a side match. In addition, the player trained in this way has high self-confidence that enables him to make good decisions.

Authors: *What does an individual training plan look like?*

RM: In individual training, you must make various different decisions depending on age, playing ability and whether the players are juniors or seniors. With the juniors, it is possible even in group training to coach players individually. Each player has a ball and can work very well in exercise forms for fast footwork and feeling for the ball. After this, the basic techniques, feints and passes can be trained. For young players, it is best to start with fast dribbling (opponent next to you) and then the turning away movements (opponent in front of you).

Children quickly achieve good results with these learned movements and can quickly implement them in many small match and training games. Later they learn the movements with the opponent behind them in order to quickly perform a feint. It often happens that the opponent is not outplayed immediately and runs with the player right to the sidelines. Then the child must learn to use other different feints in order to break free.

When I work individually with the professional players at Manchester United, we mainly train specifically from one position with certain offensive actions that the players in the team have to perform. Here, I look particularly at the 1-on-1 situation in which a certain player can perform these in his particular position. For a right back like Gary Neville, for example, I coach how he can pass into the center to transfer the attack to the other side of the pitch.

With Michael Carrick, Fletcher and Scholes, I work on turning away and opening up the game with one-twos. With the wingers Nani and Valencia, I focus on coaching the fast spotting of opponents and counterattacking, i.e., passing on the outside and pace and/or passing on the inside and fast combinations with the teammates and/or shot on goal. With Rooney, we work mainly on veering away from opponents behind him and creating small spaces where he can prepare to shoot on goal.

Authors: *What do you think of the Coerver Method?*

RM: When I read the book *The Textbook for the Ideal Soccer Player* and the foreword by Wiel Coerver in 1985, I thought, "that isn't rocket science!" The aspects of the Coerver Method make the difference and must therefore be trained in a varied way.

In recent years, a small rift has developed between the Coerver Method and many coaches, associations and bodies. These disagreements have arisen because Wiel Coerver was totally convinced of his methodology and looked critically at everything else. This in turn led to his method being viewed very critically by others. That wasn't right! It is ok to be critical, but perhaps it was just the way he communicated. In my eyes, his method is fantastic. From then on, I studied the first book and Coerver's videos in depth and could in this way understand that it is a method for complete youth coaching under the heading "technique."

With this knowledge, I have designed further training for coaches, and using a puzzle (see Fig. 43) I want to illustrate that the central theme is always technique and correlates with tactics, conditioning and mentality. That is why it is important to me that coaches know and understand the Coerver Method. They must understand that technical development is the most important thing, particularly for young players.

Authors: *What exactly do you do at Manchester United*

RM: I have been at Manchester United since 2001, first in the Academy as Skills Development Coach (SKD), later as Second Team Coach and SKD, then as SKD again and since 2007, First Team Coach. I absolutely love this job!

René Meulensteen works very closely with Fons van den Brande. The interview below with the founder of the company Sportpartners reveals the great complexity and importance of modern soccer, which no longer seems to be possible without expert knowledge.

Fig. 43:
The "René
Meulensteen Visie"
In 1 on 1 games
(Meulensteen,
unpublished

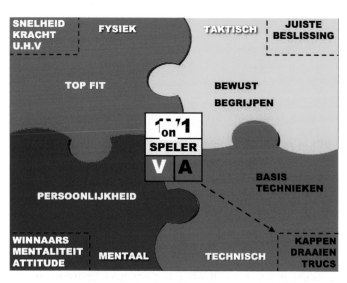

Key	
Snelheid = Speed	Kappen = Sudden change of direction
Kracht = Strength	with the ball
Fysiek = Physique	Draaien = Turning
Bewusst Begrijpen = Conscious	Trucs = Tricks
understanding	Persoonlijkheid = Personality
Juiste Beslissing = Correct decision-	Basis-Technieken = Basic skills
making	1v1 = 1 on 1
Winnaars = Winner	Speler = Player
Mentaliteit = Mentality	V = Defender
Attitude = Attitude	Top Fit = Top fitness
Technisch = Technical	A = Attacker
U.H.V. = Endurance	Tacktisch = Tactical

Interview with Fons van den Brande (Jan. 10, 2010; *Sportpartners*), Partner of René Meulensteen

Fons van den Brande (www.sportpartners.nl) was born in the Netherlands in 1956. He was, among other things, a conditioning coach at the Dutch first division club Vitesse Arnhem and for nine years was conditioning coach in the Papendal National Sports Center. In 1996, he founded the firm Sportpartners. With the help of professional lecturers, he offers advanced training in the areas of soccer technique, conditioning, rehabilitation and strength training.
The firm has branches in Belgium and the USA.

Authors: *What is the philosophy of Sportpartners?*

vdB: In recent years, the demands in soccer have been increasing constantly, so that soccer has become a gigantic marketing product. We are receiving more and more details that we perceive to be important and want to refine and optimize. Modern soccer requires players who can act multi-functionally, i.e., they can play soccer position-specifically and with fast, sports-specific footwork. Functional running and coordination training is therefore an essential component of soccer training and match play.

The increased focus on tactics always involves other aspects, too. If one plays and/or the opponent always plays against the ball because one does not want to lose and/or "keep a clean sheet," the pitch is made ever smaller and the ability for action speed in matches becomes ever more decisive with regard to:

- More 1 on 1 "duels"

- Less playing room (coordination)

- Differing individual motor skills

- The increase in starting speed, flexibility, functional coordination, reaction speed and other conditioning aspects

- Mentally "strong players" (YTDI - Young Talent Development Indicator)

- Better energy management, enabled both by a regulated deployment of energy during the match and reading of game situations on the basis of optimized conditioning

If you want to improve these points, it is not enough to increase your physical strength; you must also improve the physical components.

It is noticeable that soccer has become a powerful and complex product, in which you cannot expect the head coach to be equally knowledgeable about all performance factors. The coaching staff is a team whose work must be ongoing and detail-oriented, and as a result, an accurate yearly planning can be set up within the club structure. The educational value of running, coordination, and rehabilitation training is therefore placed in a firm framework.

Through our multicultural coexistence and also through the Bosman Ruling,[16] the clubs find that this free exchange of players with their widely differing cultural backgrounds gives rise to different soccer cultures. Every culture has its own playing style. It is expected that the coaching staff can handle this creatively and functionally so that they can get the best out of every player. The distribution of roles within the coaching staff is therefore critical. *Sportpartners* is one of the first companies to launch special courses to train these factors. It is clear to us that conditioning coaches have a highly responsible position.

Authors: *You have many lecturers on your program. What do the participants find most interesting: skills, coordination, strength, etc.?*

vdB: Our course on conditioning and rehabilitation has been running very successfully for 14 years. The skills coaching courses are the most popular. They are always fully booked because the originator (the thinker about the skills philosophy) of this subject, René Meulensteen, gives this course himself. I only work with lecturers who work at professional clubs as I think that they are working right at the top level and that their ideas can filter down into all levels. Nobody suddenly starts working at Manchester United! There is a difference between a good top coach and a good lecturer. Not everybody is able to communicate their vision. This is a discipline in itself. We think that we have lecturers who possess this quality, and we also hear this in feedback from our (former) participants.

---

16   In 1995, there was a decisive change in transfer regulations for professional players: the Belgian player Jean-Marc Bosman was playing in his hometown for FC Liège. In 1990, he wanted to leave the club once his contract had expired and play for the French second division side Dunkirk. The Belgians demanded a transfer fee of $800,000, which Dunkirk was not prepared to pay. Bosman then took legal action against the prevention of his changing clubs. After a tough legal battle, at the court of last resort, the European Court of Justice found in the player's favor on Dec. 15, 1995, because according to the EU constitution, every citizen can freely choose his place of work within the European Union. Since the so-called Bosman Ruling, players without contracts may change clubs on free transfers and furthermore there are no longer restrictions on the number of foreign players for EU citizens. For two reasons the Bosman Ruling has been strongly criticized by many stakeholders; firstly, many players ask for additional money ("bribes") for a transfer, because the clubs save money on the previously customary transfer fees. Secondly, the sheer numbers of foreigners in clubs limit the opportunities of talented local young players.

Authors: *What is your assessment of Dutch talent development with regard to technique and conditioning?*

vdB: The KNVB has not considered skills training from the point of view of Wiel Coerver and René Meulensteen. This kind of skills training has always been seen as a "forbidden fruit" in Zeist. We have jumped into this gap and are creating products so that many coaches and soccer enthusiasts – as well as parents who work in their clubs – can be stimulated by the art of soccer technique.

René Meulensteen and *Sportpartners* have trained so many coaches in recent years that when it comes to the content and methodology of this subject, we really are seen as the "godfathers" of soccer technique. That is also true for youth coaching in the area of conditioning. Here too, *Sportpartners* was the first company to see that the core skill of *flexibility* had hitherto been neglected in youth soccer coaching. We have also in the last 14 years trained a great many soccer (conditioning) coaches. In the Netherlands, there is a problem of youngsters not getting enough exercise.

Sportpartners must struggle to be able to confront the monopolistic status of the KNVB. However, we as *Sportpartners* will do our best so that our future can be a fantastic "soccer youth." Where there is hope, there is also a future.

7.5 The Dutch Goalkeeping School Using the "Frans Hoek Method"

The Dutch goalkeeping school is very closely connected with the Zeist Vision and the TIC Model. "The positional play of the Dutch goalkeepers is different from that of the German goalkeepers in that they adopt a sprinter's position and can therefore reach long balls and start a counterattack more quickly." (Schlieck, May 22, 2002). This quote shows that goalkeeping is definitely included in the basic conception of tactics with and without the ball and switching held by many Dutch clubs. That means for the KNVB that the game is the basis for every training exercise (see Den Otter, 2002, p 51). The KNVB's goalkeeping coaching plans are therefore based on the *Frans Hoek Method*. The eponymous Frans Hoek has worked intensively for more than a decade on goalkeeping in the Netherlands and has coached some of the world's best goalkeepers, including Edwin van der Saar (former Ajax Amsterdam and now Manchester United). Since summer 2010, Frans Hoek has belonged to the coaching staff of Louis van Gaal.

Frans Hoek derives goalkeeping techniques to be coached from the Dutch playing philosophy and breaks these down into two different aspects of youth goalkeeping coaching:

1. **Goalkeeping with the Ball:** reception, catching, deflecting, fisting and the abilities and skills that a field player must also learn (see Hoek, 1990, p 10).

2. **Goalkeeping without the Ball:** starting position, positional play in and in front of the goal, one and two-footed take-offs and specific falling techniques.

Dutch youth goalkeeping training content is acquired methodically through appropriate match training (specific demand profile of a goalkeeper) and team training (with field players) (see Den Otter, 2002, p 51). The following practical examples illustrate these typical features for youth goalkeeping training in the KNVB coaching plans:

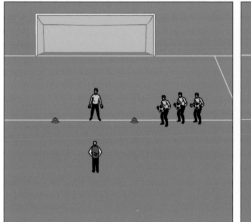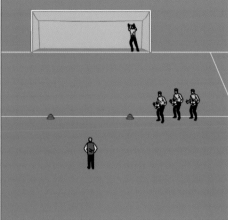

Fig. 44 and 45: Training drills to improve footwork with the ball

Procedure
On a hand signal from the coach, the goalkeeper sprints toward the goal line, stops and makes a catching action above his head without a ball.

Target and Coaching Points
Adopting the basic position, running action, turning, deflecting, catching and landing.

Variations
*   All movement directions of a goalkeeper: forward, backward, sideways, with ball.
*   Reduce and increase distance.
*   Change direction of throwing and passing (see Hoek, no year).

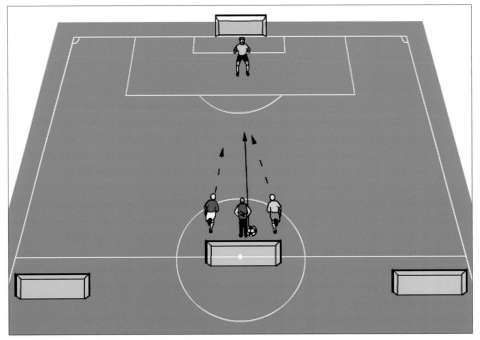

Fig. 46: Training drills to practice passing back to the goalkeeper and introduction of simple play making

Procedure

- Three goals near the center line (left, center, right) and one goal plus goalkeeper (GK) on the endline.
- 1 on 1 situation following a stab pass by the coach in the direction of the 16m line.
- GK cooperates with the defender so that one of them passes the ball accurately into one of the three goals.

Targets and coaching points

- The defender moves away to the side when the GK has possession of the ball.
- If the GK is "right-footed," he stands to the left, as the GK as a right-footer can himself accurately kick a simple volley to the right or a short pass.
- This means that the GK can turn toward the defender when he is in possession of the ball and pass to him or open up the game directly and pass into the center or outside goals.

Variations

- Head start for the defender.
- Change of direction.
- Ensure bilateral play.
- Create 1v2 and 1v3 situations.
- Speed, vary the height and spin of the stab pass (see Hoek, no year).

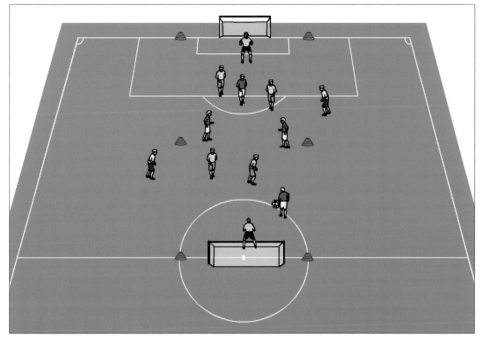

Fig. 47: Match form with emphasis on "passing back to the goalkeeper (GK)"

Procedure

- Two goals with GK in a 50m long and 15 – 20m wide pitch.
- 4v4 plus two neutral players at the sides.

Targets and coaching points

- Goalkeeper
  - Coach your team from behind, call out to the players and ask them to pass the ball back to you.
  - Take up your position to the ball.
  - Return the passed back ball to your teammates as quickly as possible.
  - If a direct pass is not possible, anticipate the ball accurately and redirect it with the next touch.

- Field players
  - Pass the ball back early to the GK.
  - Pass the ball back to the GK at an appropriate speed.
  - If possible, pass to the GK's "strong" foot.

Variations

Two additional goals are placed at the sides nest to the goals for the GK's long volleys (van Hoek, no year).

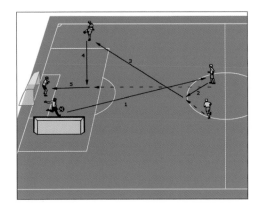

Fig. 48:
Training drill with
the emphasis on
targeted goal kick /
goal throw, intercepting
the cross, fast and
precise play making
by the goalkeeper.

Procedure

- Two wide goals plus GK (swapping places).
- Second wide goal placed sideways near the 6-yard box.
- Three teammates in one half of the pitch.

Targets and Coaching Points

- Targeted goal kick/throw to the teammate in the center.
- This player lets the ball rebound directly to his teammate on the left or right and runs behind them and rungs toward the 12-yard spot.
- The player with the ball passes to a player standing on the wing between the goal and the center line and runs directly toward the "near-side post."
- Cross toward:
  - the near-side post
  - the 12-yard spot or
  - behind the GK toward the second wide goal (far-side post).

The GK watches out for the player at the near-side post, when making a wide cross to safeguard the goal and when possessing the ball for a fast turnaround into play-making in the form of a precise goal kick (drop kick, volley, sideways kick) or throw (overhead, roll, push, sideways) to his teammates (encourage fast resumption of play depending on the situation).

Variations

- Replace the second goal with a third player.
- With opponent: GK plus 1v3 (a winger and two midfielders).
- Organize a competition
  - For every intercepted cross the GK gets one point.
  - For every direct goal by the cross players they get three points and by the midfielders in front of the goal two points.
  - For every goal after a rebound the player gets one point.
  - For a goal by the cross-players into the second goal, the players get two points (see Hoek, no year).

7.5.1 The Game is the Foundation

Interview with Thomas Schlieck (Goalkeeper Coach at German National League Club Arminia Bielefeld) About the Special Features of Goalkeeper Training in the Netherlands

A slipped disk forced Thomas Schlieck to end his playing career at the age of 26 in 1996. He has a degree in Business Administration, holds a B coaching license from the DFB and attended a KNVB goalkeeping coaching course. Since 2002, he has been responsible for the training and coaching of youth and professional goalkeepers at Arminia Bielefeld (see Schlieck, 2010, p 76-85). The authors conducted two in-depth interviews about goalkeeping coaching in the Netherlands with Thomas Schlieck on May 22, 2002 and March 10, 2010 in Bielefeld.

Authors: *What made you decide to attend a Dutch goalkeeping coaching course?*

TS: After my active career was over, I knew I wanted to continue to have an active role in soccer and train and coach goalkeepers. Purely by chance, I heard about a course for goalkeeping coaches run by Frans Hoek (then goalkeeping coach at Ajax Amsterdam) to be held at the Kaiserau Sports University in Germany. I enrolled in this course, and that's how I took the first step.

Authors: *What are the special features of KNVB goalkeeping coaching?*

TS: Goalkeeping coaching by the Dutch Soccer Association (KNVB) is run by the *Frans Hoek Sports* organization. The coaching consists of a basic course and an advanced course. The basic course is mainly concerned with the different goalkeeping techniques, while the advanced course works on tactics and is concerned with the analysis and assessment of goalkeepers and the collaboration between goalkeeping coach and head coach. Once you have successfully completed the course, you take an exam, then you are awarded a KNVB goalkeeping coaching certificate if you pass.

In the "Frans Hoek Method," the training games are the basis of goalkeeping coaching. You learn to analyze which demands the game places on the goalkeeper and which situations a goalkeeper has to master during a game.

Then we try to transfer these demands into training drills. These training drills must of course be conceived in such a way that they help the goalkeeper to improve his game. Also they must be structured so that they are as match-realistic as possible, so that the goalkeeper can recognize the situations in a match and demonstrate the required actions in those match situations. In the training situation, solutions are worked out jointly between coach and keeper. The coach constantly asks the keeper whether he thinks that his action in a training situation is correct. Particularly at the youth level, the keeper will answer "yes" or "no." The coach also asks the keeper why he has answered in this way, and by doing this, coach and keeper enter a dialogueue about the decision-making process. The purpose of this dialogueue is to encourage the keeper to think about his game and to allow him to understand why he should change things wherever possible.

Authors: *Which other goalkeeping coaching methods are used in the Netherlands?*

TS: As well as the *Frans Hoek Method*, there is also the *Pro-Goal Method* developed by Maarten Arts. This method involves the goalkeeper being proactive himself. In every situation, the keeper should gain possession of the ball as quickly as possible. One example: the keeper should spot early on that a long pass by an opponent (through the defensive chain) is likely and that he can run to the ball in front of his own penalty area and kick it back into play.

Authors: *What proportion of the Dutch goalkeeping training method do you use in your work with Arminia Bielefeld?*

TS: Dutch goalkeeping training methods form the foundation of my work at Bielefeld. My approach to goalkeeping has been aligned with that of the Dutch goalkeeping school for many years.

Particularly in youth soccer, the learning of specific skills is vital. I try to enter into a dialogueue with the keepers and to encourage them to think intensively about their game. Experience shows me that this helps to form a consistent approach that enables the keepers to use in matches what they have learned in training.

Over time, I have developed my own conception of goalkeeping coaching, which has also proven itself in practice. In addition to the Dutch philosophies, I also work increasingly more with the professional players with a goalkeeping-specific training method, with which I try to create artificial stress for the keepers during the drills. They are thus forced to perform the drills under more stressful conditions.

I am currently coaching the keepers of the professional, U23, U19, U17 and U16 squads. The work is mainly at a high performance level. Another important principle of my approach is that all keepers at the youth level should already be familiar with the drills of the senior keepers. The drills are basically the same, but there are of course differences in the number of repetitions and the speed at which they are performed. I discuss this in different ways with the keepers, so that I accompany the pro keepers every day and prepare them for all imaginable situations. I see the youth keepers once

or twice a week. The transition between the different age groups should be as smooth as possible. As soon as a junior keeper is integrated into pro training, he knows both his contact person and goalkeeping coach and also the basic drill procedures.

Authors: *What is the difference between Dutch and German goalkeeping?*

TS: The main difference between Dutch and German goalkeeping is in the conception of the game, i.e., the German approach is much more conservative. Also, in Germany, the goalkeeper's role tends to be seen as defensive, which means that the goalkeeper's position is relatively near to the goal, irrespective of the position of the ball.

In the Netherlands, it is important to teach the keepers how they should fight off these balls or solve a situation. Keepers in the Netherlands should learn which skills to use in which situations in order to be able to resolve these situations as well as possible. Already even the youngest players are familiar with kicking techniques (e.g., drop kick), and these skills are ingrained at a young age. In addition, Dutch keepers tend to think offensively. They are constantly changing their position depending on where the ball is so that they can intervene as early as possible.

8   Dutch Tactics Coaching in Theory and Practice

> "Soccer consists of different components: technique, tactics and conditioning. Conditioning, tactical skill and technique are second nature to me. There are players who are technically better than me and who may be are fitter than me, but tactics are the key and most players ignore them. Tactics can be subdivided into insight, confidence and courage."
> (Johan Cruyff, Vrij Nederland, December 1974 quoted in Barend & van Dorp, 2006, p 21).

The Dutch philosophy of tactics training is particularly targeted at the coaching of individual positions that are trained in the three phases of a game under special consideration of a maximum of tactical variability:

1. Ball possession

2. Ball loss

3. The switching process.

The 1-4-3-3 formation is still the basic structure for the development of tactical abilities and skills in the youth sections of Dutch clubs.

8.1   Classification of Tactics

Tactics in soccer can be structured according to different criteria, and are usually divided into defensive and offensive phases, and position-specific and general play.

In this context, tactics includes "a tactical procedure ... by each individual player (individual tactics), individual position groups (group tactics) and the whole team (team tactics)" (Bisanz & Vieth, 2000, p 48). These individual and collective activities are introduced from the perspective of *one position*, so that it is obvious if one's own team is in possession of the ball or not. The position-specific perspective of the tactical actions in Dutch soccer is explored in more detail in Chapter 8.4.1.

In the following paragraphs, we do not aim to go into great detail about individual, group and team tactics in particular but to describe changes in tactics training in general (see te Poel, 2009, ps 83 – 88). Here, we attempt to outline the tactical features of Dutch youth soccer training:

- *Individual tactics:* Van Lingen (2001, p 174) terms the "1 on 1 in space" as the nucleus of Dutch youth soccer, it represents the individual tactical means of defense in top level soccer, in order to gain possession of the ball. Danny Blind (May 8, 2003) underlines this classification and stresses that youth players in training must often be put into tackling situations in order to improve positional play and tactical defensive understanding in direct comparison with the opponent. In the 1-on-1 situation, the defensive player should always position himself on a line between his own goal and the attacking player while standing sideways so that he can watch the ball and the player. Individual tactics are, according to Blind (ibid), closely linked to situation and experience anticipation. According to Michels (2000a, p 158), for the offensive player in a 1-on-1 situation, the maintenance of ball possession and/or shooting on goal are always central to his individual tactical behavior. Michels (ibid) emphasizes that the formation with three strikers in youth soccer would be a playful way of soliciting and encouraging "offensive" individual tactical behavior in the 1 on 1 in particular. In the training process, this formation is closely connected to technique training with and without the ball. Dribbling, passing, feinting, ball reception and running with the ball, making oneself available for a pass and running into a space are the basics of combination play, confronting the opponent, putting pressure on the opponent (vertically/-diagonally), barging, shooting on goal, tackling.

- *Group Tactics:* In line with the Dutch youth soccer training philosophy, group tactics in even and uneven sided games are based on individual tactical skills in attack, defense and when switching in both directions that must now be agreed with by one's teammates (see van Lingen and Pauw, 2001b, p 50) through communication and coaching (see Chapter 5.2). In offensive group tactics (with possession of the ball), according to van Lingen and Pauw (ibid), the targeted teamwork in small groups of players is important. However, the automatization of the basic technical principles is a prerequisite for successful combination play. Offensive play can be practiced in even and uneven-sided games, and in the Netherlands, the objective of group tactical offensive play is met by using uneven-sided training games that allow players at least two passing possibilities. The possibility of passing to the "third man" reflects the Dutch philosophy of "always creating at least two open men" that allows new, alternative ways of continuing the game.

- *Team Tactics:* Every group tactical behavior represents the basis for the tactical actions of the whole team. All actions should be structured so that the opposing team is prevented from playing a flowing game, "or in other words: *the anti-soccer process must work*" (Michels, 2000a, p 69). In Dutch youth soccer, the switch from ball loss to ball possession is seen as an important criterion for an effective team performance. According to Biermann and Fuchs (1999, p 99), the Dutch playing style is characterized by "each of the ten field players being attackers as well as defenders." Ideally, a team that is tactically coached in this way can create different and unanticipated pressure on the opponent in the most diverse playing situations, which makes the team play with variety and creativity and sometimes unpredictably. Team tactics in general means the planned actions of all players on the team in possession of the ball. Secure play-making, counterattacking, game shifting and wing play represent elements of team tactics. According to Michels (2000a, p 90), these team tactical elements are based on comprehensively and intensively coached individual and group attacking methods within a team. Only then can offensive players perform them effectively and accurately at high speed. Dutch coaching does not consider wide and pitch-opening passes to be an effective offensive measure. On the contrary, all team members should participate in combination play that should be characterized by short, quick passes (*circulation soccer*) (ibid, p 91). "High balls into the opposing half are frowned on because their chances of attacking success are too dependent on chance" (Hyballa, p 2003b, p 23).

8.2   The 1-4-3-3 System

A playing system should, according to the Dutch coaching philosophy, be the foundation for unified team actions. Thus, the whole team participates in every formation in both defense and attack. According to van Lingen (2001, p 171), the formation represents the way in which the players work together. Therefore, also according to van Lingen (ibid), the choice of formation in the Netherlands is also somewhat dependent upon the specific characteristics of the available players and the playing rules in force. New formations, such as the 1-4-4-2, 1-3-4-3, 1-3-5-2, 1-4-5-1, 1-4-1-4-1 or 1-4-2-3-1 are always responses to rule changes in the history of soccer development (e.g., the off-side rule).

In the 1966 World Cup, Sir Alf Ramsey developed the 1-4-3-3 formation. The English national team played this system with a so-called "sweeper" in front of the defense, and the German national team refined this in the 1972 European Cup to a 1-4-3-3 formation with a *libero*, who played behind man-to-man-marking defenders, but who could push into the midfield if he gained possession of the ball. At the 1974 World Cup in Germany, the Dutch national team used a formation whereby they exchanged man-marking for zone-marking in order to be able to play more flexibly and creatively (see Biermann & Fuchs, 1999, p 101). Since then, this formation has dominated in the Netherlands and is frequently taught and played in youth soccer. "In youth coaching, the 1-4-3-3 system has become a Dutch national treasure" (Kormelink, 1999, p 14).

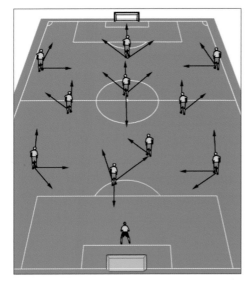

How does this Dutch 1-4-3-3 formation work in practice?
The 1-4-3-3 formation (see Fig. 49) comprises the following elements, which are given numbers that in the Netherlands stand for the exact position of the players and their different tasks on the pitch.

Fig. 49: The 1-4-3-3 system according to the Dutch model (see Hyballa, 2003a, p 17)

In the Dutch literature, number one usually refers to the goalkeeper. That means that the goalkeeper is considered to be an integral member of the formation (see Chapter 7.5).

- Four defenders – a right back (number 2) and a left back (number 5), a central defender (number 4) and a "free man" (number 3), who plays in front of, behind or level with the back three. These elements are sometimes referred to in the literature with other numbers (e.g., number 5 swaps with number 3) (see Fig. 49 and Tomaz, 2007, p 10).

- Three midfielders – a right (number 6), a left (number 8) and a central midfielder (number 10).

- Three strikers – a right (number 7) and a left-winger (number 11) and a center forward (number 9).

The 1-4-3-3 formation is now practiced all over the world, but it is sometimes organized slightly differently. In 2003, the German U17 team played (see Fig. 50) "with a back four, two defensive central midfielders, one offensive midfielder, two wingers and a central striker" (Stöber & Peter, 2003, p 22).

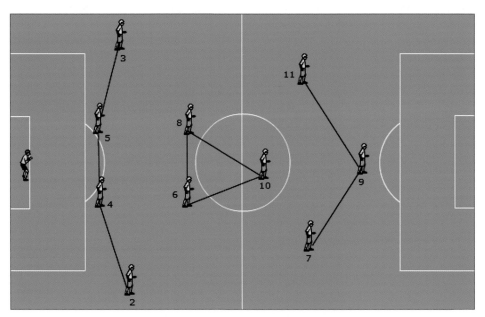

Fig. 50: 4-3-3 formation (DFB U17 formation 2003) (ibid, p 25)

If we now compare the Dutch 1-4-3-3 formation in figure 49 with the DFB U17 from 2003, we can see that the Dutch formation has a more offensive orientation, as the "free" defender (number 3/4) can switch from defense to attack.

According to the Dutch model, every player in the 1-4-3-3 formation is aware of position-specific tasks (see Chapter 8.4.1) that he must fulfill in a tactically disciplined but creative way. The width and depth of the zones on the pitch "owned" by each player are all the same size. As in every formation, there are players whose aptitudes make them more defensively or more offensively inclined (or vice versa). In the German version of the 4-3-3 formation from 2003 (see Fig. 50), the four defenders are arranged in a chain formation. However, in the Netherlands, three defenders play together with a "free" man. "The free man decides for himself how he plays. He has total freedom and is therefore the most important player in the defensive formation" (van Amstel, Jan. 28, 2003).

The Dutch youth philosophy prioritizes offensive soccer with effective, short passing so that play-making by the defense in particular should be very purposeful. According to Kormelink and Seeverens (2001, p 7), with possession of the ball, "more play-making variations are possible with four defenders." In this formation, with the help of the different position groups and the technical method of short passes, the ball can be moved forward purposefully from the defense via the midfield into the forward's area. This *short-passing offensive soccer* from the team's own half requires that all players form *triangles* so that the player with the ball always has two passing options. The build-up and adoption of the triangle, repeated many times across the pitch, enables the team (from goalkeeper to midfielders) to move the ball up the pitch under control, safely and accurately, and represents the foundation for swift and direct offensive play (see Hyballa, 2002a, p 53). The forming of triangles not only guarantees the players an advantage when attacking but also when playing defensively. Under the concept of "ball-oriented pressing" (see Chapter 8.4.2), the Dutch youth players are taught in their tactical training in the 1-4-3-3 formation how to behave off the ball. This formation always gives defenders and midfielders the possibility of passing wide or deep to a midfielder. These ready-made "passing points" should ensure that:

- No long runs forward from the defensive areas of the pitch are required
- The offensive positions (6, 7, 8, 9, 10 and 11) have many passing options when in possession of the ball (see Fig. 49)
- Both wide and deep **short** passes are equally possible

As the players on the wing adopt the outside positions, there is good presence down the width of the pitch. Based on the positions of the free man, central and midfield defenders and center forward on the pitch, the ball can also be passed deep in a sequence of short passes (ball circulation within each position group) (see Dusseldorp, Seeverens & Vergoosen, 2001; Boudeweel, 2002, p 17). *A kick and rush* (play making with long balls) is therefore not an acceptable tactical solution.

The chosen formation should also help the players save energy. This means that the technical-tactical performance factors are prioritized in the Dutch coaching system. Seen in this context, it is easy to understand the often-quoted statement by Dutch coach Louis van Gaal: "Running is for animals. Soccer is all about brain, ball and opposition." (van Gaal, 1.9.2010a). Young Dutch players are therefore not expected to run a lot, but to play a lot of soccer (see also Dusseldorp, Seeverens & Vergoosen, 2001). As can be seen when observing training and matches at SC Heerenveen, the young players get an accurate and thorough instruction in the 1-4-3-3 formation (see ibid; Hyballa, ,2003a, p 17).

The 1-4-3-3 formation thus meets two key objectives in Dutch youth coaching:

1. The technical and tactical core skills, including their position-specific features, are priorities of Dutch youth coaching.

2. The Dutch "soccer mentality" is consistent with the offensive 1-4-3-3 formation (see Heising, 5.20.2003; Schulze-Marmeling, 2010, p 83-90) and enables the youth players to develop both individual creativity as well as active and purposeful participation in all defensive and offensive areas of the match, even if they do not always win their matches.

8.3   The Four Main Phases of Tactics Training

Using the 1-4-3-3 formation, the KNVB divides the course of the soccer game into four main phases. According to the Dutch soccer philosophy, the team works as a whole in these four phases, as a "total team" (van Lingen, 2001, p 174). That means all youth players in the Netherlands, in training and matches alike, are permanently involved in play making, and in both offensive and defensive play. In Germany, this approach to the game is known as "total soccer" (Biermann & Fuchs, 1999, p 100).

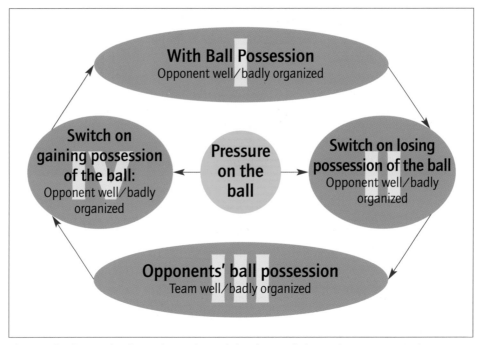

Fig. 51: The four main phases in tactics training (Kormelink & Pabst, 2002, p 27)

As can be seen from Figure 51, the **first main phase** of every soccer match begins **with ball possession** (see also Dusseldorp, Seeverens & Vergoosen, 2001). In this phase, the attention of the team and coach is directed to the opposing team's organization, as it should be the objective to "break up" the organization of the opposing team "and to bring the ball and as many players of your own team behind as many opposing team players as possible" (Kormelink & Pabst, 2002, p 26). In order to be able to implement these intentions, the young players are coached and trained to be able to put pressure on the opposing team's defense with effective short passes and few touches. When the players adopt their positions in the zones, both deep (in the center) and wide (in the outside positions), they can pursue their aim of moving quickly toward the goal and scoring, while bearing in mind that they "do not play long passes if it's not appropriate" (van Lingen, 2001, p 159). In the phase of ball possession and play making, the Dutch youth players are required to look around them and be aware of what is going on upon the pitch. At this point, the interweaving of tactical training with the contents of the TIC Model (see Chapter 4.2.1) becomes clear: the solution of match situations by means of technique, *intelligence* and communication. This game intelligence is particularly evident in Dutch positional play, as the players must fulfill certain position-specific tasks in their offensive play (see Chapter 8.4.1).

The **second main phase** of the soccer game is characterized by the **switch on losing** possession of the ball (see Kormelink & Pabst, 2002, p 27). When ball possession is lost, your team determines the future course of the game with the aim of quickly regaining possession of the ball. The solution to this problem can be achieved by positioning as many players as possible on the now-defending team behind the "ball line," i.e., between the ball and their own goal. This usually reduces the available passing space in the width and depth of the pitch. The Dutch youth players therefore learn the strategy of defense in zonal defense. This tactical method on loss of ball possession requires the players to immediately adopt defensive basic positions. "Thus switching over according to the principle of 'short paths'" (Kormelink & Pabst, 2002, p 27). That means that every player adopts the position near where he finds himself in each game situation, thus giving rise to a ball-oriented shifting of all players on the entire pitch.

If this approach is not successful, the **third main phase** kicks in, which is the organization of the team **when the other team has the ball** (see Dusseldorp, Seeverens & Vergoossen, 2000). In this main phase, the zones are tactically reduced and the team shifts to the *side of the pitch where the ball is*. The purpose of space reduction is to restrict the other team's effective strategies, such as targeted and fast passing, fast dribbling, crossing, diagonal balls behind the defense and shooting on goal, so that at least the playing speed and rhythm are slowed down and passing paths are blocked. In this phase, coaching (see Chapter 5.2) acquires particular importance, because the teammates *behind* the front players should give brief and precise instructions as to which zone is effectively defended. "At Vitesse Arnhem, even the kids have to learn to communicate with each other. They must understand that from a tactical point of view, particularly when defending, it is more effective to coach on a technical level. Coaching for us also means helping" (Edward Sturing, March 13, 2003). If effective "pressure on the ball" is exerted in this phase, the defending team usually regains possession of the ball, thus moving directly to the **fourth main phase, switching on gaining possession of the ball** (see Petersen, 2001, p 23).

Sturing (March 13, 2003) assumes that for the team with the ball, *patterns in the other team's zonal positioning* are obvious, so that the other team's lack of organization, i.e., many opposing team players are situated between the ball and the other team's goal. A fast or securely executed counterattack can follow this situation analysis.

In the **fourth phase**, the visual perception of the players (according to the Dutch playing philosophy) should always be directed down the pitch so that they can destabilize the opposing team's disorganized defense with a pass into the potential goal-scoring zone. This requires excellent timing and self-confident decision-making with regard to the assessment of the risks involved (see Kormelink & Pabst, 2002, p 27). In the Netherlands, youth coaching focuses on the above four main phases, because almost inevitably, in training and matches these phases are intertwined so that the two main switching phases (first and fourth) in particular predominate. As the players get older, the coaching content is expanded to include position-specific tactics training within a playing system.

8.4   Special Features of Dutch Tactics Coaching

The term *total team* is at the heart of the Dutch youth coaching philosophy. *Total team* stands for the permanent participation of the whole team in all actions, both defensive and offensive. This approach requires that the youth players in particular can classify the typical Dutch *positional play, training games for pressing and kaatsen (rebounding) and set pieces in zonal defense and team-tactical play making* and understand their meaning.

8.4.1   Position-Specific Tactics Training

On the basis of the abovementioned understanding, the Dutch youth coach lays the foundations for the players to be able to fulfill clearly defined tasks set by the coach more and more autonomously. The training drill of positional play represents for Kormelink and Seeverens (1999e, p 40) the optimal training method with which to theoretically and practically clarify the tasks and functions of the youth player within the total team. "Positional play is an excellent method with which to coach circulation soccer" (ibid). These training drills are derived from the 11v11 match. As a result, in training, the young players play in the position that they also adopt in matches. The youth players therefore learn the special tactics of their playing positions and can concentrate on solutions in position-typical game situations in attack and defense.

Below we analyze the different position groups in the 1-4-3-3 formation with and without possession of the ball from the Dutch perspective:

What characterizes a **Dutch youth goalkeeper** is his training with regard to communication with his teammates. His position on the pitch allows him to see all position groups so that he learns to "read" different situations. Goalkeepers in the Netherlands therefore learn the technical abilities and skills of passing, shooting on goal, ball reception and running with the ball, dribbling and the visual perceptual abilities (spotting free space) alongside the "classical goalkeeping techniques." When his team is in possession of the ball, the keeper should step forward out of his goal so that other players can pass to him as the free man usually moves forward on the offensive. As the keeper in the Netherlands participates in the game, he also possesses the abilities and skills of a field player, and these abilities and skills are part of the demand profile of the Dutch youth goalkeeper (see Chapter 7.5.1).

The **free man (3)** and the three **defenders (2, 4 and 5)** form the defensive line-up in the 1-4-3-3 that must close up when the other team has the ball. The nearer the other team gets into the defensive center along the central axis of the pitch, the more the three defenders (2, 4 and 5) should focus on the ball and try to reduce the "offensive space" of the other team's front row.

The main task of the free man (3) consists of being able to make autonomous decisions in game situations. For example, he must decide whether when faced with a "free" player from the other team in the center of the pitch who is not yet under pressure/- marked, whether to move in front of or behind the defensive row. Therefore he should have above-average knowledge of:

- The four main tactical phases
- The necessary abilities and skills of the position
- The position groups of his teammates and the other team
- His own strengths and weaknesses
- The situation and experience anticipation

in the area of practical abilities and skills, secure positional and build-up play is expected. This allows an optimal pitch coverage (Sturing, March 13, 2003). Like the goalkeepers, during the build-up, the free man also needs to be able to communicate well with all those participating in the game on the pitch because in the game build-up he must make quick, accurate decisions as to whether he goes directly into attack or remains behind the defenders.

The distribution of the three defenders (2, 4 and 5) when their team has the ball is along the width of the pitch so that the playing space in the sense of a secure build-up can be extended, "but in the back of their minds, they must constantly be thinking about what happens if they lose the ball" (van Lingen, 2001, p 178) and also learn to think defensively when they do have the ball.

The positions of the midfielders in the 1-4-3-3 formation are divided into **right** and **left outside players (6 and 8)** and **central midfield player (10)**. If the other team has the ball, the three midfielders must go back on the defensive. Positions 6 and 8 should "block" the direct path to their goal, the center. Both outside players therefore shift following the ball, thus greatly reducing the other team's playing space.

Position 10 represents a kind of "controller" in this phase because he possibly should block the other team's forward free man. If the other team has the ball, the three midfielders play in a line. Positions 6 and 8 therefore occupy the width and depth of the pitch. They always play behind the attacking players and should work on creating scoring opportunities that they can convert from a distance via shots on goal (see Dusseldorp, Seeverens & Verdoossen, 2001).

Both wingers **(7 and 11)** and the **central striker (9)** form the forward line in the Dutch 1-4-3-3 formation. The three forwards should always defend as a group. When the other team has the ball, they retreat back to the midfield zone, thus again reducing the other team's playing space. The three forwards are responsible for the other team's four defenders by virtue of their positions on the pitch. It is obvious that the three forwards cannot be directly responsible for the four opponents (2, 3, 4 or 5). The forwards defend in their prescribed "zone" and should primarily prevent long passes from the rear zone into their own half (see van Lingen, 2001, p 178). If the forwards have the ball, their job is to score goals. In this regard, the job of the wingers is first to adopt the outside positions so as to open up again the playing space for their own offensive players ("widen the pitch!"). The *central striker* looks for a way into the center of the other team's half of the pitch and makes himself available for long passes from/through the forward-placed midfielder (see Hyballa, 2002b, p 32). *Making yourself available, running free and crossing* are the basic prerequisites for taking this position (playing without the ball). Understanding and mastering these group tactical measures opens up possibilities for the forward-moving midfielders to push forward by fast dribbling into the previously opened up spaces (gaps) and make direct shots on goal. To play in this way, forwards need to know and understand the abovementioned tactical principles in addition to being able to run very fast, tackle well and develop excellent skills (dribbling, shooting on goal, crossing and heading).

The positional play games (*positiespel*) required for the practical transfer of the training of the positions within a team, which can be included in the coaching levels from C juniors onward, requires answers to the following questions: how can I pass the ball in a certain situation and position, or block a pass (tactical intention) and which technical abilities and skills (technical intentions) do I have? In these ways, the ball is not only passed precisely, quickly and with variety and creativity, but the passes (the technique) are combined with a specific intention. In training, this combination should lead to a combination of choosing and implementing a position-specific technique (e.g., precise,

flat and quick pass) and a tactical aim (e.g., push pass into an alley) as an efficient unit. In this way, the Dutch also want to counteract a development-specific stagnation in the area of technical abilities and skills. "Ongoing training activities will stop them deteriorating so that at least a stabilizing of the technical skills can be achieved" (Kormelink & Seeverens, 1999b, p 71). The Dutch believe that this stabilization can be achieved by positional play games.

The **positional play games** selected below are intended to illustrate the transfer into training practice.

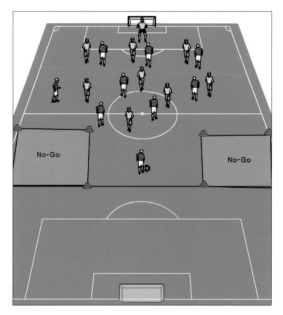

Fig. 52:
Long ball and "no-go zones"

Procedure

- Play 9v8 on three quarters of the pitch with a wide goal and goalkeeper.
- In opposite corners of the pitch, mark out two 20m x 20m "no-go" zones with cones.
- The bigger team plays into the wide goal, and in their play making must not dribble or pass through the no-go zones. Aim: to encourage the long ball.
- The smaller team tries to dribble over the line between the two no-go zones.
- They should prepare this dribbling with long balls and may also use the no-go zones.

Coaching

- Hard and precise passing game.
- Make space for the long ball!
- The bigger team plays well together and lets the ball run by forming triangles.

Variations

- The bigger team receives restrictions (depending on their ability) in the number of ball touches.
- The no-go zones are removed.
- Place another wide goal between the no-go zones.

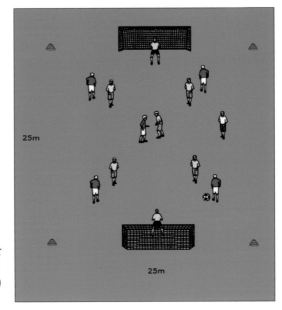

Fig. 53:
5v5 plus 1
(triangular game [driehoekspel])

Procedure

- 5v5 plus 1 on a 25m x 25m pitch with two wide goals plus goalkeepers.

- Both teams play a 2-1-2 formation (symbolizes the diamond formation).

- The team with the ball tries, together with the neutral player, to constantly form new triangles.

Coaching

- The player with the ball always needs two open men.

- Close down the spaces when you lose the ball, and increase them when you win the ball.

- The neutral player should mostly stay in the center in order to make the ball "fast."

Variations

- The neutral player has only one touch.

- Place mini goals on either side of the wide goals.

- Ask for flat passes. As soon as the ball gets too high, the game is stopped and the other team gets to restart the game.

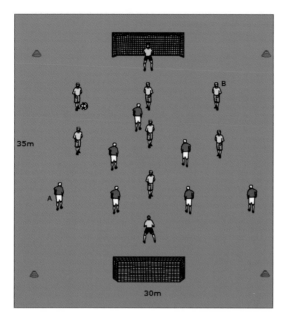

Fig. 54:
Positional play (positiespel)
7v7 with time limit

Procedure

- On a 35m x 30m pitch, two teams play into two wide goals with goalkeepers.

- Team A is offensive and uses a 3-3-1 formation, and team B is defensive and plays with a 4-2-1 formation.

- Team A must gain a two-goal advantage within 8 minutes, otherwise team B has won.

Coaching

- Fast switching after losing possession of the ball (coaching by the GK).

- Immediate staggered retreat back down the pitch after losing possession of the ball (keep the center stable).

- Keep the ball speed extremely fast.

- The players without a ball only anticipate the ball from a preliminary action.

Variations

- The coach decides that team B is in the lead at 2:0. Team A is placed under time pressure.

- The coach discusses certain moves with each team separately beforehand. If a goal is scored by one of these certain moves, this team gets two points.

- At higher level: reduce the size of the pitch and only allow "one touch soccer" *(Een Contact Voetbal).*

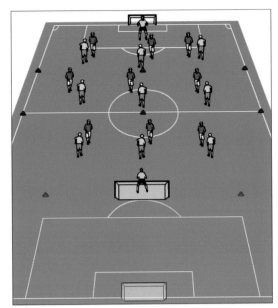

Fig. 55:
Positional play (positiespel)
9v9 with set pieces
(spelhervattingen)

Procedure

- 9v9 on three quarters of the pitch with three zones into two goals with GK.
- Both teams play using a 3-3-3 formation.
- After a *careless* ball loss in the offensive zone: throw-in for the other team (from position determined by the coach).
- After a *careless* ball loss in the center zone: corner (coach determines from which side of the pitch the corner is taken).
- After a *careless* ball loss in the defensive zone: free kick (from position determined by the coach).

Coaching

- Quick ball circulation *(balcirculatie)*.
- Fast footwork when passing to the player without the ball.
- Fast counterattack after winning the ball after set pieces.
- Form a triangle for throw-ins, study free kicks and corner kicks

Variations

- As soon as the ball reaches the central zone, the ball may no longer be passed backwards.
- As soon as the ball reaches the offensive zone, the players have four seconds (depending on ability) to score a goal.
- Alternate between games with free play and games with one touch.

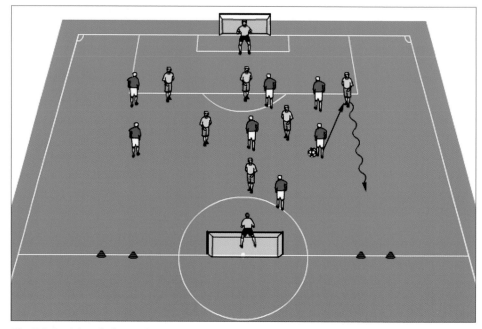

Fig. 56: Positional play 7v6

Procedure

- Play 7v6 on half a pitch into two goals with GK.
- On one end line, set up two more cone goals (2m wide).
- The bigger team plays with a 1-3-3 formation. The smaller team plays in a 3-2-1 formation.
- The smaller team counterattacks after winning the ball toward the wide goal, or tries to dribble through a cone goal.

Coaching

- Fast but safe ball circulation from the bigger team.
- The smaller team involves their GK to secure the ball.
- The smaller team forces the team with the ball outward, "away from the goal!"

Variations

- Set up an even-sided game (6v6, 7v7).
- The bigger team may only score from 8m away from the goal: "play combination soccer right up to the goal!"
- If the smaller team retains possession of the ball 5 times, it gets an extra point.

8.4.2 Playing Drills for "Ball-oriented Pressing"

Ball possession is very important in the Netherlands, so their youth coaching tries to emphasize the formation of a high *attacking zone*. This means that at the first cross by the opponents, the players should and/or could attack, with the distances between the "pressing" players always being very short. The focus of this tactical measure should be immediately gaining possession of the ball but **not** clearing the ball. Gaining possession of the ball should then be followed by a quick switching phase involving the team restructuring for the ensuing offensive formation, producing *offensive and dominant play*, even against the ball (see Chapters 6 and 11).

The training games below show how pressing is practiced in the Netherlands.

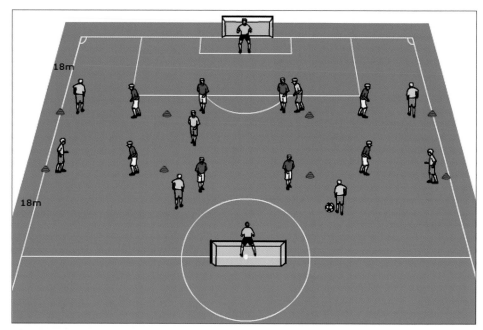

Fig. 57: 8v8 with forechecking

Procedure

- 8v8 on half a pitch and two wide goals with GK. 18m in front of the goals there is a line, which is used for "offensive pressing" *(pressie)*.
- The defending team must push forward and put the players participating in the game build-up permanently under pressure.

Coaching

- Attack early.
- The "back men" must run into the spaces so that no ball can be passed through them.
- Run to, evaluate and "press" either to the center backs or right and left backs on the coach's instructions.

Variations

- As soon as the GK passes the ball forward, the team that wants to press has only 5 seconds to gain possession of the ball. Otherwise, the players participating in the game build-up get an 11m advantage.
- The forechecking zone is divided into inside and outside zones to identify which players should be pressed.
- The players participating in the game build-up lead 3:1, and the coach allows play to continue for 3 more minutes.

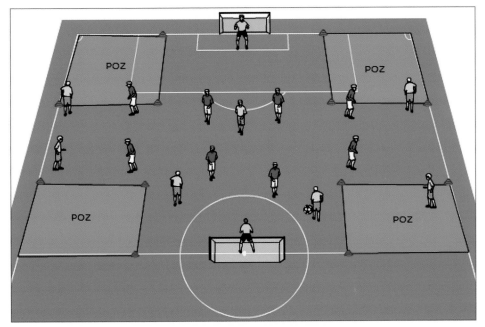

Fig. 58: 7v8 with special Pressing Zones (PZ): "Press outwards!"

Procedure

- Play 7v8 into two wide goals with GK.
- Mark out two special pressing zones (PZs) on the wings in front of the goals.
- The bigger team is the "pressing" team. It must try to force the team with the ball into the PZs. If they succeed, the team gets a bonus point.

Coaching

- Guide the attack outward.
- Don't "close down" the outside back straight away.
- Run laterally up to the center backs so that they must also pass the ball into the PZ.

Variations

- Play with even-sided teams.
- The first ball from the team participating in the game build-up must be passed into the PZ. If the pressing team doesn't then gain possession of the ball, the team with the ball gets an 11m advantage.
- The coach calls out into which PZ the attack should take place (encourage situational pressing).

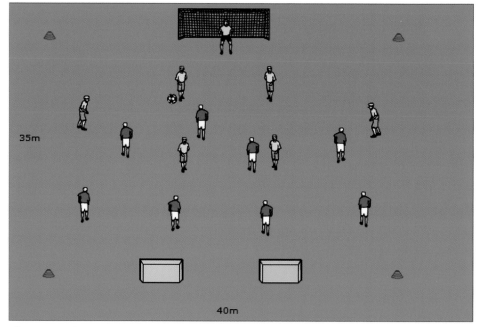

Fig. 59: 6v8 into a goal with GK with a specific scoreline: "pressing under time pressure!"

Procedure

- Play on a 35m x 40m pitch with one wide goal with GK.
- At the other end of the pitch, place two small goals without GK.
- The bigger team plays into the wide goal with GK.
- The smaller team counterattacks into the two small goals.
- The smaller team must always build up the game.
- The bigger team is losing 1:3.

Coaching

- Don't run to the outside too fast in the pressing situation.
- The gaps behind must be filled quickly.
- The players on the bigger team can also use two men to press the player with the ball.

Variations

- Time limit of 3 minutes.
- Whenever the bigger team scores a goal, the smaller team loses another player.
- Whenever the bigger team scores a goal, it receives a player from the smaller team.

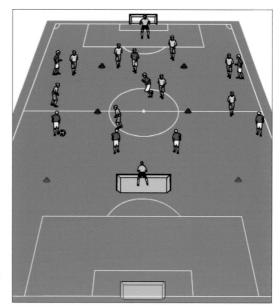

Fig. 60:
8v8 with pressing in the center:
"Offensive defense in
the center!"

Procedure

- Play 8v8 on three quarters of the pitch with two wide goals with GK.
- Mark out a zone in the center of the pitch to be used for orientation purposes by the players and coach.
- The defending team of eight should perform a pressing into the center.
- The outside backs should be marked in order to make the center "tight."
- The ball should be guided into the center.
- If the pressing team gains possession of the ball, it may pass it along to the goal.

Coaching

- Alternate midfield and offensive pressing.
- The ball can also be "stolen" from behind.
- Arrange outside backs so that the central players are forced to run through the center.

Variations

- Play 8v10.
- If the pressing team wins the ball, play continues normally!
- Remove the zone but still continue to press into the center.

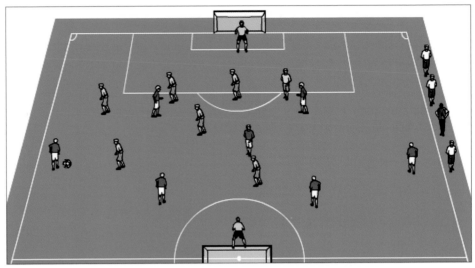

Fig. 61: 7v7 with three extra pressing players: "create outnumbering situations!"

Procedure
- Play 7v7 on half a pitch and two wide goals with GK.
- The coach stands with three neutral players on the edge of the pitch.
- The players play 7v7 in a tactical formation.
- In every situation that he considers to be a pressing opportunity, the coach can send in the three players.
- He can send in the three players together or one after the other.
- The neutral players reinforce the defending team.
- The coach can take these neutral players off the pitch at any time.

Coaching
- As soon as one team outnumbers the other, they press!
- Provide lateral security.
- Loud coaching from the "men at the back."

Variations
- The coach chooses a captain who shouts out when the substitute players must be sent on and off the pitch.
- Play 4v4 on a narrow pitch. The trainer coaches 10 substitute players outside the pitch.
- If the smaller team can keep the ball for 8 seconds, the pressing team loses a point.

8.4.3 Playing Drills with *Kaatsers*

Another typical Dutch manner of combining technical and tactical coaching elements are *training games with kaatsers* (rebounds). In the Netherlands, direct rebounds are used:

- If you are closely marked and cannot even shake off your opponent by feinting, one-touch play is introduced (*"een contact"*).

- To allow fast combination soccer.

- To speed up the game with flat pass soccer.

- To enable well-timed passes into free space (and running).

- To create geometry for faster game shifting and to form triangles.

- To encourage playing to a third player.

- To coach fast one-twos, particularly in the midfield.

- To open up the playing zones at the back and the outside.

- To look for the most direct and fastest path to the goal ("long ball").

The training games below practice rebounding and should enable these elements to be implemented.

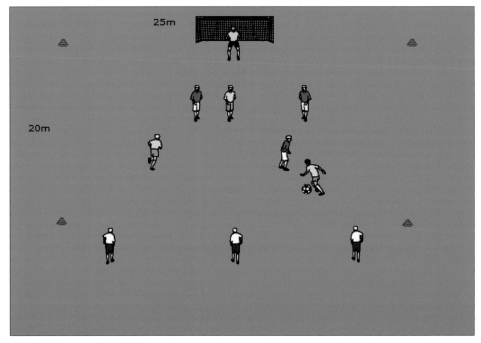

Fig. 62: 3v3 with three kaatsers

Procedure

- In a 25m x 30m pitch, play 3v3 with a wide goal with GK.

- Three neutral players (*kaatsers*) stand behind a line of cones opposite the wide goal.

- The *kaatsers* may only pass the ball with one touch; there is no touch limit for the players in the 3v3.

- The *kaatsers* always play with the team that has the ball so that there is always a 6v3 situation.

Coaching

- The neutral players are always on the move.

- Don't provoke any unnecessary tackles when attacking.

- Also ask the *kaatsers* to play the "killer pass," i.e., a pass into the player's path.

Variations

- The neutral players are flexible and run around the pitch.

- Ask for "triangular play." The ball should not be passed back to where it came from.

- The ball may only be passed flat.

Fig. 63: 4v4 with two kaatsers

Procedure

- See Fig. 62, except that the two neutral players play on the wing.
- The neutral players *(kaatsers)* pass the ball with only one touch.
- The *kaatsers* may initially only pass the ball flat, but later may also pass it high.

Coaching

- Ask the players to play to a third man.
- Play precise, hard and flat passes.
- Shoot on goal as soon as there is a gap in front of the goal.

Variations

- One neutral player moves around the pitch while the other remains on the wing.
- The field players may only play with one touch, but the *kaatsers* are not limited; slow the game down.
- A goal scored after a skillful "three-way play" scores two points.

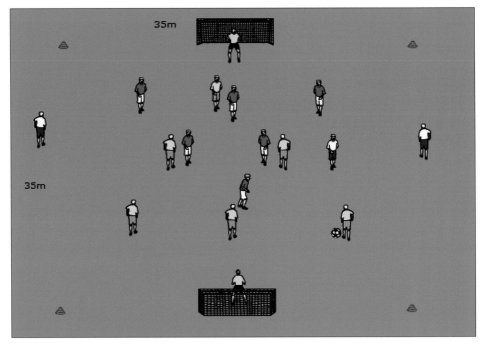

Fig. 64: Positional play 6v6 with three kaatsers

Procedure

- Play 6v6 on a 35m x 35m pitch with two wide goals with GK.

- Both teams play a 3-2-1 formation.

- One *kaatser* moves around the pitch (as a neutral player), and also one neutral player plays on each wing.

- All neutral players play with the team that has the ball and are only allowed one touch of the ball.

Coaching

- If play gets too narrow, open it up with a pass to the wing.

- Ask for fast one-twos in the center.

- The mobile neutral player always stays in the center.

Variations

- The neutral players should shoot on goal from the wings.

- The three neutral players move around the pitch.

- The neutral players only pass the ball forward.

8.4.4   Playing Drills for Set Pieces in Zonal Defense

How can your team play set pieces with good spatial distribution against the ball without the players on the defending team running after every single attacking player? Dutch soccer coaching is very concerned with zonal marking in general and this question in particular, which in the Netherlands is answered using this example of defensive play during corner kicks:

- Think like a striker, watch the ball (not the man) and "go into" the ball.
- Avoid blocking.
- Keep the gaps between you and your teammates very short.

The following situation-related set piece form should help to implement this perspective into training practice.

Procedure

- Play 6v6 into two wide goals with GK.

- Place balls ready to be thrown in along the sidelines.

- Play 6v6 in a specific tactical formation.

- If a throw-in is imminent, the first throw must be thrown to the GK and the second to allow play to continue.

Coaching

- The GK catches the ball at its highest point.

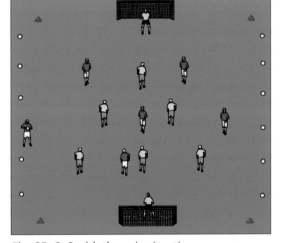

Fig. 65: 6v6 with throw-in situation

- The GK pushes his teammates forward to give himself enough space.

- The GK also waits for the second ball.

Variations

- Instead of throw-ins, try this exercise with free kicks and corners.
- The GK fists the first ball.
- After a save by the GK, his team gets one point (to boost motivation).

8.4.5   Playing Drills to Open up the Game

As can be deduced from the above, opening up the game *(Opbouw van Achteruit)* represents a kind of key element in Dutch youth coaching, particularly because the systematic game build-up in general does not correspond to the spontaneous way kids play. Goalkeepers and defenders often tend to play long balls in free play, in order to:

• Reach the other team's half quickly.

• Set up running duels for their own strikers.

• Be able to keep the ball and their opponents as far from their own goal as possible.

This type of play is not in line with the Dutch coaching philosophy, which is particularly characterized by ball possession with many ball touches and "passing relays," several action alternatives and inspiring, offensive team play (see Chapter 6). The two training games presented below help to introduce a purposeful game opening by the goalkeeper and the defenders.

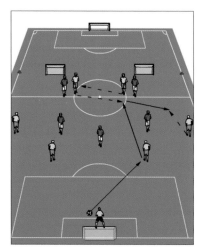

Fig. 66: Small-sided game; 6 plus GK v 5 (with reference to the 1-4-3-3 formation)

Procedure

• One team plays with 6 players plus goalkeeper with one wide goal with GK.

• The other team consists of 5 players who defend two small goals placed to the side.

• The aim is the improvement of the game build-up and the free play of one of the two outside backs.

Rules

• Free play.
• The bigger team starts to open up the game and shoots into the small goals.
• The smaller team tries to counterattack into the wide goal.
• If a set piece arises, the GK gets the ball and a new game opening develops.

Coaching

• When the GK has the ball, the outside backs stand "wide." The center backs also spread out in the center.

• The GK passes to the center backs, who pass to the outside backs via a midfield player.

• The midfield player approaches with a preliminary action. After letting the ball rebound, he runs directly to the new position and makes himself available for a diagonal pass.

- When the long ball is played to the midfielders, the outside backs run into the free space.

Variations

- The coach can vary the size of the pitch according to the players' ability.

Procedure

- Play with two teams and two wide goals each with a GK.
- One team plays with 8 players, the other with 7.
- In both defensive corners of the smaller team, mark out a no go zone with cones, thus making the pitch narrower.
- The aim is to improve game opening and free play by the outside backs.

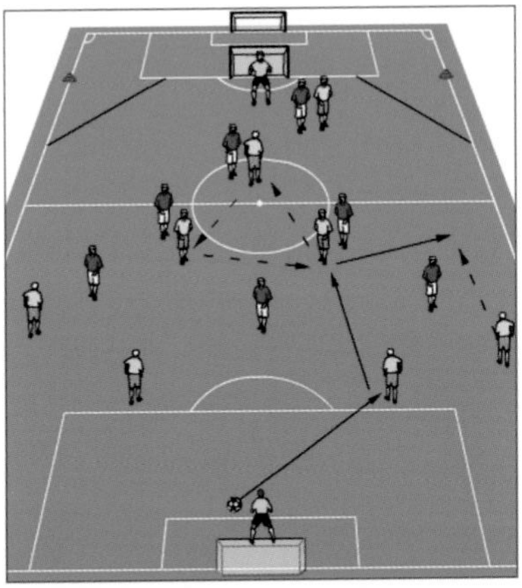

Rules

- The bigger team tries to play the ball long, so that the outside backs can play freely.

Fig. 67: Game build-up (part 2) – 8 plus GK v 7 plus GK (with reference to the 1-4-3-3 formation)

- The outside backs should not play crosses from the free space, but dodge out onto the wing and end the playing situation with a flat pass or a 1 on 1.
- If there is a set piece for the bigger team, the game is started again by the GK of the bigger team and a new game build-up starts.

Coaching

- When the GK has the ball, the outside backs stand wide so that the center backs move together. The midfielders stand deep!
- The GK passes to the center backs, who again passes to an outside back via the midfielders.
- The midfielders then change positions if the outside backs win the ball. The midfielder farthest from the ball approaches and the midfielder nearest to the ball goes deep.
- After the midfielder's pass, he looks for a new position and asks for a diagonal pass.
- The ball is in the center and the outside back sprints into the free space.

Variation

- See Fig. 66.

8.4.6 Playing Drills for Team Tactics

Game solutions in a game between two teams are largely dependent on the formations used by each team. Particularly when different formations are playing each other, varied and creative teamwork by all players is essential (see Fig. 68). In The Netherlands, therefore, small-sided games are often used that require and encourage solutions by means of provocation rules and/or other methodical measures that can be match-determining. They are therefore visualized for the players and coach in training so that another coaching objective, mutual coaching, can also be optimized within a match (see Chapter 5.2).

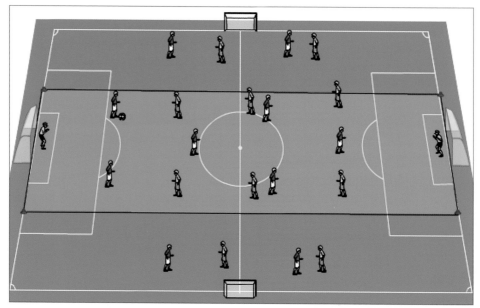

Fig. 68: 1-4-4-2 against 1-4-3-3 ("point backward" [see Chapter 6.2]) with narrow one-touch zone

Procedure

- On a large pitch, play 10v10 into two wide goals with GK.
- Place two small goals halfway up the sidelines without GK.
- Between the two wide goals, mark out a 25m wide zone (one touch zone). In the narrow corridor between the two goals, only one touch is allowed to enable quick long passes.
- Play 1-4-4-2 against 1-4-3-3 ("point backward" [see Chapter 6.2]).
- Free play is allowed down the wings near the two small goals.
- Goals may be scored in the wide goals (= three points).
- Goals may also be scored in the small goals (= one point).

Coaching

- Never pass the ball straight in the one-touch zone if your teammate has still not shaken off his marker.

- Loud coaching in the one-touch zone.

- Sometimes also play a targeted pass to the "second row."

Variations

- The two small goals are removed.

- Wherever three consecutive one-touch passes are played, one goal counts three points.

- 1-4-3-3 ("point forward" [see Louis van Gaal in Chapter 6.2]).

- The ball should only be played with one predetermined foot in the one-touch zone (practice kicking with the inside and outside of the boot).

9   Dutch Conditioning Training in Theory and Practice

Soccer – a physical game of chess?

> "It's a mental game. It is not about running all over the pitch and wearing yourself out, although of course you have to work hard. Every Dutch player wants to control the game. We pass the ball from man to man and wait for a gap."
>
> (former Dutch national team player Arnold Mühren; quoted in *Winner*, 2008, p.194)

According to van Lingen (2001, p 159), many young players associate conditioning training with pain, exhaustion and long-distance running.

It is universally acknowledged that conditioning (composed of strength, speed, flexibility, agility and coordination) is a key performance component in the soccer training process. Outstanding technical abilities, skills and tactics are not enough to play successfully in modern high performance soccer. As technical-tactical performance factors are seen as the dominant variables in the Dutch coaching system according to their training philosophy (see Chapter 8.3), it is necessary to analyze how, when and in what proportion to the other performance components conditioning training should be carried out in the different developmental stages and levels of Dutch youth coaching (see Verheijen, 1997, p. 232).

9.1   The Zeist Vision and the Special Features of Conditioning Training

The concept of conditioning is not considered to be a standalone part of training in Dutch youth soccer, but instead is considered in relation to all other performance components and, as a result of this philosophy, a kind of "hybrid" is used in youth soccer training. "Conditioning training is soccer training, soccer training is conditioning training" (van Lingen, 2001, p. 159).

In the Netherlands, from the C juniors onward, conditioning abilities are improved through soccer-specific training drills, including game and match forms. According to van Lingen (ibid, p 160), soccer-specific conditioning is developed using this method.

The Zeist Vision firmly situates conditioning ability in the whole training process and in every training session, so every junior training session always involves playing soccer.

Van den Brande, director of IAPF Holland (2002, p 27), stresses that running and conditioning training for soccer players should always be seen and structured from the perspective of the game (see Chapter 7.4).

This Dutch philosophy of conditioning training can be clarified by five typical examples:

- "Soccer conditioning" (see Chapter 9.1)

- Soccer-specific endurance ability using the training game 5v5, i.e. GK plus 4vGK plus 4 (see Chapter 9.2 and 9.2.1).

- The interval shuttle run test (ISRT) of Dr. Raymond Verheijen (see 9.2.2).

- Soccer-specific coordination training (see Chapter 9.3).

- Youth conditioning training of Harry Dost (conditioning coach at Twente Enschede) (see Chapter 9.4).

Chapters 9.1 and 9.2 in particular offer training that consists of high conditioning loads and demands are combined with the development of technical and tactical abilities and skills.

According to van Lingen (2001, p 164 and 176), the Dutch playing philosophy should primarily teach youngsters in the D and C juniors all types of movement experience in order to improve endurance abilities. This approach is usually retained in the older juniors (B and A juniors) according to the motto, "The body follows the mind" (ibid, p 164). Understanding the game of soccer is an absolute priority in Dutch youth coaching and follows the TIC model (see Chapter 4.2.1), which situates soccer playing into a learning process because "the greater the TIC, the better the conditioning" (van Lingen, 2001, p 159).

It is obvious that the initial quote by Arnold Mühren and the reference to the quote by Louis van Gaal (2010a), "running is for animals," can only be correctly interpreted if one knows and takes into consideration the synergistic approach of the Dutch coaching philosophy.

The example training games below should show how the abovementioned understanding of Dutch soccer conditioning can be put into practice during training.

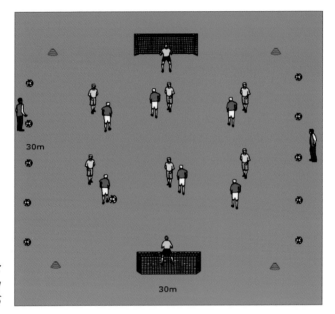

Fig. 69:
Soccer conditioning
training 6v6

Procedure

- Play on a 30m x 30m pitch with two wide goals with GK.

- Both teams play in a 1-3-3 formation.

- Extra balls are placed along the sidelines. Coach and assistant coach also stand along the sidelines.

- Half the pitch is marked out with cones.

- A goal is only scored when all players, except the GK, are situated in the other team's half.

Coaching

- Move quickly and a lot without the ball!

- Try to form triangles.

- After the replacement ball is thrown onto the pitch by the coach/assistant coach, the players should switch quickly.

Variations

- Increase the size of the pitch (emphasis – endurance).

- Reduce the size of the pitch (emphasis – speed).

- Replacement balls are thrown immediately, almost automatically into the pitch.

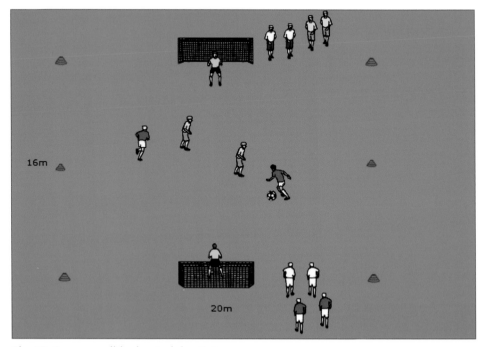

Fig. 70: Soccer conditioning training 2v2

Procedure

- Play 2v2 with two wide goals with GK.

- Pitch: 20m x 16m

- The team of two that scores retains possession of the ball and continues playing.

- The GK quickly returns the ball to the pitch. The other team of two swaps places with another team of two that is waiting behind the goal.

- If no goals are scored after 30 seconds, four other players come onto the pitch.

- Playing time: about 12 minutes, including changes.

Coaching

- Work progressively against the ball.

- Always stand close together (short distances between the players).

- Loud and effective coaching of the teammates.

Variations

- 2v2 with four neutral players who spread themselves out on the pitch.

- The coach adds additional players so that 3v2, 4v2, 4v3 can be played.

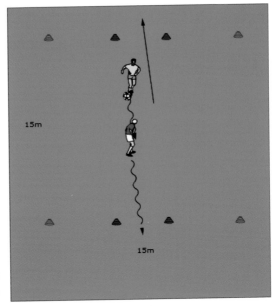

Fig. 71:
1 on 1 development of
"dueling strength"

Procedure

- Play 1 on 1 into two small cone goals (right and left).

- Pitch is 15m x 15m.

- The player can shoot into one side of the cone goal; on the other side, he must dribble past the other player.

Coaching

- The defender must block the other player's path next to the goal he intends to shoot into. He must defend the other goal that must be dribbled through in a lunge position to slow down the opponent.

- Ask for 1 on 1 (offensive) at full speed.

- Aim for effective feinting movements.

Variations

- Play 1 on 1 into two wide goals with GK.

- Play 1 on 1 into two small goals with GK.

- In a 1 on 1, the players must always be very alert. They must never dribble backwards (thereby taking the pressure off).

9.2 Soccer Conditioning: Soccer-specific Interval Training by Dr. Raymond Verheijen

"Soccer conditioning" is developed by playing soccer. The correct stimuli must be given at the correct time" (Verheijen, 2009a, p 26). Based on this premise, which is very reminiscent of the typical features of the Dutch philosophy of soccer conditioning training mentioned in Chapter 9.1, the Dutch conditioning coach Dr. Raymond Verhiejen, under the guidance of Head Coach Guus Hiddink, began the three-week preparation training (periodization) of the Russian national team for the European Cup in 2008. This was preceded by practical experiences of dealing with the different target-performance comparisons with regard to "soccer conditioning, regeneration and explosive capacity" (ibid, p 29):

- Conditioning coach of the Dutch national team at the 2000 European Cup (with Frank Rijkaard; semi-final) and 2004 (with Dick Advocaat; semi-final).

- Conditioning coach of the South Korean national team at the 2002 World Cup (with Guus Hiddink; fourth place) and Australia in 2006 (with Guus Hiddink; last 16).

In addition, Verheijen implemented his model of soccer conditioning at FC Barcelona (Spain), Feyenoord Rotterdam (The Netherlands) and, since 2009, at Manchester City (England).

By monitoring heart rate in the Interval Shuttle Run Test (ISRT) (see Chapter 9.2.2), Verheijen was able to establish (compared to the already known values in senior European elite soccer and available UEFA statistics) a significant lowering of heart rate after high loading with a loading end after 15- and 60-second recovery breaks with all players on the Russian national team at the start of the European Cup 2008. During the European Cup 2008, this led to "our players, even in the semi-final, being able" to run and often sprint (ibid, p 32). The Russian team reached the semi-finals of the 2008 European Cup.

Training drills that improve soccer conditioning (ibid, pps 30-31) included 1 on 1 (see Fig. 72), 1vGK (special training, see Fig. 73), 1v0 plus cross to two forwards (see Fig. 74), 3v3 plus 2 GK (see Fig. 76), the 4v4/5v5 plus 2 GK (see Fig. 75) and 7v7/8v8 plus 2 GK (see Fig. 77) with a ball and two goals plus goalkeepers.

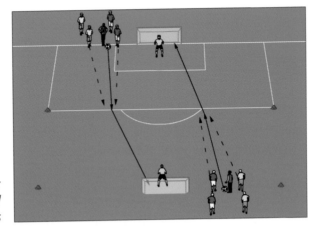

Fig. 72:
1 on 1 – maximal
explosiveness

Procedure

- Doubled penalty area with two wide goals and GK.
- Pairs of players for the 1 on 1 stand to the right and left respectively of each goal; between them is the coach/assistant coach with the ball.
- Measured, straight push pass toward the center line.
- Both players run after the ball to shoot on goal.

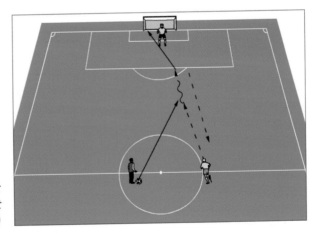

Fig. 73:
1 on 1 to the ball – sprint
endurance (special training)

Procedure

- The coach/assistant coach stands with the ball about 10m behind the center line.
- The coach passes in the direction of the goal with the goalkeeper.
- The player sprints behind it, receives the ball at high speed and shoots on goal as soon as possible.
- He then trots back to the starting line.
- The coach adapts the training load to the players' coaching level and training objective.

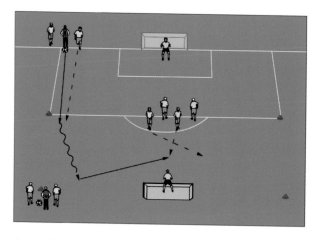

Fig. 74:
Explosiveness endurance:
sprints with few passes

Procedure

- Two cross-pass players stand next to each other opposite the penalty area.
- 2x2 attacking players stand in the center (short-long; crossing).
- The coach or assistant coach plays a straight stab pass forward.
- Sprint to the ball and fast dribbling toward the end line with cross or back pass to each "point" player.
- The coach adapts the training load to the players' coaching level and training objectives.

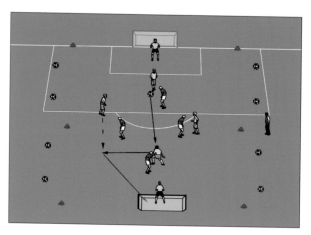

Fig. 75:
4v4 plus GK/5v5 plus GK

Procedure

- 4v4 plus GK/5v5 plus GK on a 40m x 30m pitch with two wide goals.
- Both teams play in a diamond formation in order to try to stick together as much as possible when running.
- Place plenty of replacement balls near the sidelines and the goals.
- The coach adapts the training load to the players' coaching level and training objectives.

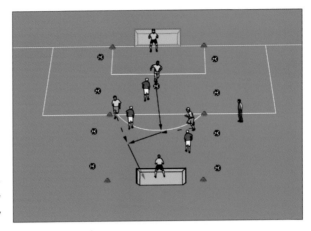

Fig. 76:
3v3 – "high speed
and fast recovery"

Procedure

- 3v3 plus 2 GK in two wide goals on a 30m x 15m pitch.
- Ensure fast playing pace.
- Have replacement balls ready (see Fig. 75).
- The coach adapts the training load to the players' coaching level and training objectives.

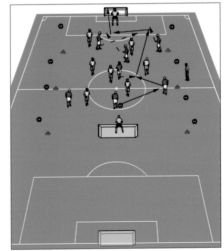

Fig. 77:
7v7 plus GK/8v8 plus GK –
recovery endurance

Procedure

- 7v7 plus GK/8v8 plus GK in two wide goals on an 80 x 40m pitch.
- Play several run-throughs with short rest breaks.
- Ensure a fast playing pace.
- Have replacement balls ready (see Fig. 75)
- The coach adapts the training load to the players' coaching level and training objectives.

Dr. Raymond Verheijen presented his approach to soccer conditioning during a BDFL advanced training course for coaches and sports scientists in German and discussed it under the heading "Do you train traditionally or correctly?" (Verheijen, 2009b, p 6-14) (see Chapter 9.2.3). It would exceed both the scope of this book and miss the point if we now presented Verheijen's precise model of periodization in great detail. Instead, the authors would prefer to note that according to Dr. Verheijen's presentation (2009b, p 12), it is precisely in the area of youth soccer that many talents are lost because "young players ... are not (author's note) introduced to training gradually! To start with, therefore, training should be less intensive and shorter, just a few minutes' playing. If professionals train six times per week, then youngsters should only train four times!" For Verheijen (ibid, p 12), soccer conditioning with the ball is part of a long-term plan, which requires a slow build-up with special focus on technical-tactical training sessions instead of the search for transitory success. For the authors, this aspect again indicates that Verheijen is striving for a consistent philosophy of soccer training and coaching in the Netherlands, which is always as match-realistically oriented as possible, and from this, the training content and methods are consistently derived. In this way, the Dutch philosophy of soccer conditioning and explosive capacity remains the common theme between the Zeist Vision, the TIC model, the Hoek Goalkeeping School, the 1-4-3-3 formation and the periodization model (at senior level), in which the duration, content and intensity of training loading must be given special consideration in youth training.

9.2.1   5v5 Playing Drills (Verheijen & Hiddink)

5v5 training games (GK plus 4vGK plus 4) are played on a 40m x 30m pitch in a diamond formation, which allows pitch coverage to be wide and deep. Plenty of replacement balls are placed along the sidelines and in the goals, thus ensuring that the players run as much as possible. To allow as many players as possible to perform the same number of running repetitions, this kind of "team periodization in training games" (Verheijen, 2009a, p 30) can also be organized in tournament form on two pitches (e.g., 4-minute load [with high intensity] and 3-5 minutes rest). According to Verheijen, this training game allows the coach:

*   To observe the game carefully.

*   To control the volume and intensity of the load.

*   To carry out situation-appropriate changes with regard to the technical-tactical emphases (uneven-sided games and 8v8 with a corresponding increase in pitch size [see Fig. 77]).

*   The channeling of the youngsters' natural movement behavior, which is characterized by frequently spontaneous, intermittently very intensive and explosive movement (oscillating movement pattern).

*   To incorporate motivation and fun in the form of small-sided games.

In addition to periodization and supercompensation (see Hottenrott & Neumann, 2010, pps 13 and 19) for young players, the authors want to use Verheijen's example of high-performance soccer to show that the coaching of soccer conditioning from basic training to high performance training can (2009a and b) be trained fully with the ball and appropriate training games, so that the:

- Sports-motor objectives of the Dutch coaching philosophy
- The development of technical and tactical abilities and skills including the sufficiently flexible application in the interaction of teammates and opponents
- The development of action speed

continue into performance and high-performance training with no changes to either content or methodology. "Conditioning training is soccer training, soccer training is conditioning training" (van Lingen, 2001, p 159), which can be implemented internationally. The circle completes itself.

9.2.2 The Dutch "Interval Shuttle Run Test (ISRT)": A Conditioning Test for Soccer Players

In the Netherlands, talented young players are guided carefully and with consideration to physical and psychological developmental phases to achieve optimal soccer results at the high-performance level.

Internationally, there are different ways of directly and indirectly measuring performance and development, and to predict performance in the core skills of soccer technique, tactics and conditioning.

Technical skills
a   Direct: recording successful and unsuccessful actions.
b   Indirect: battery of technique tests.

Tactical skills
a   Direct: numerical assessment of actions (i.e., participation in game build-up).
b   Indirect: battery of tactics tests.

Conditioning skills
a   Direct: recording of running performance.
b   Indirect: battery of conditioning tests.

These are described in details in technical literature where their application in youth soccer is discussed (see in particular Verheijen, 1997, Raab, 2001, Memmert & Roth, 2003, Weineck, 2007, pps 75 – 89).

The Interval Shuttle Run Test (ISRT) was developed at the Institute of Human Movement Sciences of the University of Groningen in 1998 (see Dolleman, 1998) and supplements the existing interval run tests (Shuttle Run Test and the Yo-Yo Test). It was tested and endorsed by Lemmink, Verheijen and Visscher (2004, p 233-239) in particular for its soccer-specific value "for measuring endurance in a more soccer-specific way" (ibid, p 233). Since 2009, the ISRT has been available on CD, accompanied by an in-depth manual explaining how to use it (see Universitair Centrum ProMotion Groningen, 2009). The authors believe that this test is also consistent with the Dutch philosophy of soccer conditioning, which is highly oriented to the interval-like nature (a-cyclical aerobic endurance) of the game, but without a ball. The players perform "running periods at a specific speed in stages of about 30 seconds with active rest breaks (slow jogging) of 15 seconds..." (ibid), (see Fig. 78). The running back and forth is carried out at distances of 20m with a fixed protocol for a steady increase in speed, which is indicated by "beeps" on the CD. It starts off at 10km/h, and increases by 1km/h every 90 seconds. From a speed of 13 km/h, this increases to 0.5 km/h. The result is produced by the number of times the 20m distance is run. The test can be carried out in groups and also offers the possibility of remaining at a sub-maximal level. German national league clubs now train with interval running (e.g., Mainze 05 under soccer coach Thomas Tuchel) (Pfeiffer, 2010, 21) with the "Yo-Yo Test" of Dr. Jens Bangsbo. The authors believe that the ISRT could be used in youth coaching.

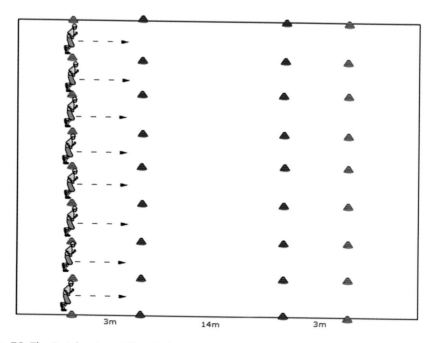

Fig. 78: The Dutch Interval Shuttle Run Test (ISRT) – a conditioning test for soccer players.

However, despite their practical experience with the test as a supplementary monitoring and training method, testing in the areas of effectiveness and reliability for youth performance soccer is still lacking (see Hoff, Kähler & Helgerud, 2006, p. 116 –124; Meyer & Faude, 2006, pps 147 – 8). Taken as a whole, new research findings in kids' and youth sport show the positive effects of intensive training methods on the endurance and strength performance abilities of children and youth. These effects can be achieved in a comparatively short time. With short, intensive training loads with appropriate rest breaks, there is no danger of overloading the cardiopulmonary system. Another factor is that, irrespective of the type of intensive loading (strength or endurance), children's regenerative capacity is greater than that of adults. However, there is also another urgent need for research into the impact of intensive training on children's bodies in order to critically evaluate the partly predominant schools of thought from the 1970s and '80s, and to give priority to time-efficient high-intensity training (see Hebestreit, Mimura & Bar Or, 1993, pps 2875-2880; Helgerud et al., 2007, pps 665-671).

9.2.3 For and Against Soccer Conditioning with Particular Reference to Modern Integrative Approaches (of Erik ten Hag [co-soccer coach at PSV Eindhoven] and Andreas Schlumberger [DFB])

The contributions of Dutch coaches Dr. Raymond Verheijen (2009a and b) were intensively discussed on fußballtraining.com and at a training course for German Soccer Coaches (Westfalia Association) under the heading "Soccer Conditioning Training" on April 26, 2010 at the Kaiserau Sports Center. In Kaiserau, Dutch coaches Erik ten Hag (co-coach at PSV Eindhoven)[17] and Andreas Schlumberger (DFB conditioning coach) supported Dr. Raymond Verheijen's approach to soccer conditioning and made their very comprehensive presentations available to the authors. The authors have identified the advantages and disadvantages of Verheijen's soccer conditioning training method, with regard to its used in youth coaching, from the "exchange of opinions" on fußballtraining.com, in which 17 soccer experts from amateur soccer, the DFB training center and professional soccer participated, and also from the BDFL CPD courses in Kaiserau and from August 2–4 in Düsseldorf and a current contribution on the practical implementation of the ideas of Dr. Verheijen in the U19 high-performance areas of the German national soccer league (see Barez, 2010, pps. 40-53).

---

17 Erik ten Hag is a former pro player and assistant coach who was head of the FC Twente Enschede Soccer Academy. He is famous for developing his own "training periodization and fitness philosophy" and in this has brought together content building blocks of both the Netherlands and Germany. In his publications and articles, Erik ten Hag writes about sports philosopher Jan Tamboer, who understands intentional movements as necessary solution-related activity (see Tamboer, 1979).

Advantages

- There is a direct connection with soccer. "Conditioning abilities in soccer have a direct connection to specific movement coordination"[18] (Schlumberger, April 26, 2010).
- Attractive and motivating conditioning training with the ball.
- The gradual increase in loading for youngsters is possible.
- Avoidance of overloading and injuries.
- Takes into consideration the scientific training principle of progressive loading increase.
- The changes between maximal explosiveness, maximally fast recovery, explosiveness endurance and the retention of fast recovery are shown.
- Technical and tactical abilities and skills are considered to be key elements in the coaching of a talented young player destined to become a professional player.

Disadvantages

- Excessively narrow pitch dimensions and the consequent promotion of playing long balls.
- In the long run, similar loading stimuli, particularly in the area of acceleration and sprinting speed (maximal explosiveness), do not lead to further improvement of these performance features (see also Erik ten Hag, April 26, 2010).
- A gradual increase of loading volume and intensity leads to a performance limit (see ibid).
- The importance of extensive-regenerative endurance runs for regeneration and endurance-maintaining training methods is not discussed.
- The lack of targeted individualization (including isolated training drills for sports motor core skills) with regard to the management of effort and regeneration throughout seasonal changes (see also ibid).
- The subsequent implementation of soccer-specific forms limits speed (see ibid). All three areas (1) specific movement coordination "games," (2) basic coordination "multidirectional movement behavior," and (3) running, must be trained (see Schlumberger, 2010).
- There is no reference to the use of standardized strength tests.

The advantages and disadvantages listed above show that conditioning training in soccer can be placed on a continuum between the poles of exclusively standardized and objective performance monitoring and the subjectivity of the coach's eye. In between, experts refer to a range of hybrids with and without the ball. It would therefore

---

18   Andreas Schlumberger (DFB conditioning coach) placed the emphasis on movement coordination and economy as the basis of soccer-specific fitness training in his presentation on "fitness training" with the DFB juniors. Like Erik ten Hag, he considers the target of fitness training to be a 90-minute optimal performance readiness for all soccer-specific movement sequences.

definitely be very beneficial for the further development of international youth soccer coaching if sports science could examine more closely the monitoring and effectiveness of training models, in particular in the sensitive area of build-up and continuation training. In this vein, the BDFL hosted an cutting edge international exchange of opinions and ideas at its "International Coach's Conference 2010" in Düsseldorf under the heading "Current Trends at the 2010 World Cup – Soccer-Specific Conditioning Training" (see also Pfeifer, 2010, pps 20-21). *New scientific building blocks* for the analysis of the issue of loading and effort monitoring in youth soccer should also be included. By way of example, we should also mention the "Four-Step model" of the adaptation of conditioning abilities (Hottenrott & Neumann, 2010, pps 13-19), "HIT" (High Intensity Training), "The effect of different recovery protocols after high intensity interval training" (Hägele et al., 2009, pps 10-14), the "Evaluation of running distances in different speed areas in professional soccer" (Braich, Brauch & Mester, 2008, pps 8-12) and Stiglbauer's (2010) empirical study about HIT in soccer.

9.3   Soccer-Specific Coordination Training

Today, from an exercise science perspective, it can be clearly stated that specific conditioning training represents "not stereotypical, boring or mindless repetition of movements, but ...a motivating and concentrated, varied activity" (author's note) (Neumaier, 1999, p 87). Dutch talent coaching, and in particular the so-called *Ajax School* (Ajax Amsterdam, 1996), had anticipated early on that in soccer, good coordination is required in order to "achieve flexible and harmonious transitions between running and technique requirements" (Hyballa, 2000, p 41). In the 1990s, the trainers of the Ajax school were already working very intensively on specific running and coordination training in their integrated coaching philosophy (see Chapter 10). Already coaching   the F juniors, Ajax Amsterdam realized very early on that "two-footedness on the part of the F players of Ajax is the most important thing" (van Veen & Smink 2003, p 36) and could be effectively supported at a grassroots level through supplementary training.

All over the world, conditioning training is now included in the basic training of youth soccer (see Kröger & Roth, 1999) in the form of ball coaching that is:

- *Playful situation-oriented* (involving teamwork, asking for the ball and orientation, playing the advantage and opponent restriction).

- *Ability-oriented* (particularly time pressure, accuracy pressure, variability pressure, complexity pressure and loading pressure).

- *Skills-oriented* (making oneself available, observing paths, controlling angles and effort).

They do not only train the coordinative abilities and skills, but also aid general tactical and technique. In matches and in practice, these approaches are used to pursue the following objectives:

- Learning to play in "pure" games with tactical demands (ibid, p 13).
- Improvement of ball coordination in the practice of general demands (ibid).
- Improvement of basic ball skills by practicing technical demands (ibid).

In this way, the performance level in the areas of technique and tactics can be improved.

In preliminary, transitional, performance and high-performance training, it often assumes the function of *coordinative supplementary training*, in which it is particularly used to optimize certain key performance components (e.g., frequency speed) for the prevention and rehabilitation (e.g., balance training combined with stabilization training, see Schreiner & Thissen, 2008) and "Life Kinetik" to optimize perceptual and decision-making processes in soccer (see Lutz, 2010) either in isolation and/or in complex form.

In the Netherlands, the youth sections of the professional clubs (e.g., at PSV Eindhoven, Twente Enschede and Ajax Amsterdam) in particular have been working with this kind of training for several years (using specially trained running and coordination coaches) to supplement general soccer training (see Hyballa, 2000, p 37). Today, these additional training measures are included in every weekly training plan and are also supplemented by cross training in such activities as Judo and gymnastics. In the narrower sense, they are not consistent with the Zeist Vision of the KNVB. As they have now gained worldwide publicity and are now part of the curriculum of all soccer talent coaching, examples for training practice are unnecessary at this point.

9.4 Development-specific Youth Conditioning Training at FC Twente Enschede

The coaching at 2010 Dutch Champions FC Twente Enschede is summarized below as an example of a development-specific youth conditioning training in a Dutch national soccer league club.

For years at FC Twente Enschede, conditioning training for the pro players and youth players has been masterminded and implemented by Harry Dost (see Dost no year,: ibid, no year). In the past, Harry Dost worked with the German head coach Hans Meyer and the Dutch head coach Fred Rutten. In the 2009/2010 season, under the English head coach Steve McClaren (2010/2011 Head Coach VFL Wolfsburg), he was responsible for the development of conditioning at FC Twente Enschede. On many occasions, Harry

Dost has published examples of his conditioning work with talented youngsters in the Netherlands. The contents below have been compiled based on the brochure produced by Harry Dost titled "Koordination im Fußball" (March 30, 2003).

Harry Dost divides conditioning training into the familiar sports motor core skills, relates them to certain developmental levels and always places flexibility, speed, strength and endurance in training practice in relation to *coordination and agility*. For this reason, he places the emphasis of his coaching on the combination of these two core skills, which he considers to be particularly important for the coaching of young talents.

Harry Dost advocates a short *warm-up program* consisting of stretching exercises and active flexibility exercises. He places special value on a dynamic stretching program for talented young players in puberty (see te Poel, 1987, pps 3-9).

In the 10-11 years age group, Dost focuses his training work on the development of *speed* (see te Poel & Eisfeld, 1987, pps 3-7). The spatial and temporal orientation abilities should at this point be developed using drills with posts and tires.

Between the ages of 12 and 18, Dost emphasizes *strength and stabilization exercises*, which he combines with forms of ball control.

From the age of 15 onward, he starts at FC Twente Enschede with a targeted *jump school*, which he combines with forms of speed training and ball skills. Dost also refers to this emphasis as complex training, which he uses extensively at this developmental stage of the youngsters.

The performance component *endurance* is not trained in isolation in the training practice of FC Twente Enschede, but is developed in extensive and intensive form in training games, in line with the philosophy of soccer conditioning (see Chapters 9.1 and 9.2).

The following overview gives firm guidelines regarding the development of the essential sports motor core skills (for each age group) necessary for the training of talented youth at FC Twente Enschede (see Dost,March 30, 2003).

Development of Strength in Talented Youngsters at 2010 Dutch Champions FC Twente Enschede

5- to 6-year-olds

Target: It is too early to talk about specific muscle strength. Functional strength can be developed by improving general coordination.

Exercises: Hopping and little jumps over low hurdles. No endurance loading.

7- to 9-year-olds

Target: The further development of functional strength by increased movement experience. Speed and jumping strength can be improved slightly.

Exercises: Hopping and little jumps over low hurdles. No endurance loading.

10- to 11-year-olds

Target: The improvement of strength capacity. The improvement of speed develops parallel to the increase in speed strength.

Exercises: Hopping and bounding over and next to hurdles. Two-legged jumps. No series. Make training fun by using training games.

12- to 15-year-olds

Target: The specific differences between the sexes in the development of strength start to become evident. Girls have two thirds of the strength potential of boys. The difference in strength is maximal between the ages of 14 and 15.

Exercises: Stabilization exercises for the hips and particularly for the abs and back muscles.

Jumping load: 6-8 x hops on left and right legs; 6 - 10 x bounding; 6 x hops over small hurdles.

From the age of 15

Target: Both maximal strength and speed strength increase in boys, as well as strength endurance. From this period onward, strength endurance should be trained. The basic techniques for specific training (and strength training) can now be performed. Strength development in girls stabilizes.

Exercises: All kinds of jumping and stabilization exercises.

Development of Endurance Performance in Talented Youngsters at 2010 Dutch Champions FC Twente Enschede

5- to 6-year-olds

Target: Endurance exercises with low intensity. Playful exercises are possible.

Training games: Endurance loads of one minute (e.g. 4 x 1 minute) followed by short breaks.

7- to 9-year-olds

Target: The aerobic endurance performance capacity increases. The priority is pace awareness and movement technique. Loads should be developed in playful exercises. The "active" rest breaks are longer than 2 minutes.

Training games: From about 4 x 2 minutes or 3 x 3 min or 2 x 4 min or series with 3 min – 3 min – 2 min or 1 min – 2 min – 3 min – 2 min – 1 min loading duration.

10- to 11-year-olds

Target: Further increase in aerobic endurance performance. Adaptations of the cardiovascular system are possible with systematic training. Improvement in running ability as a result of improved running technique and pace awareness. The following loads are recommended (rest break length should be greater than 2 minutes):

Exercises: Given in minutes: 5-4-3-2-1 or 4-3-3-2-2 or 5 x 2 min or 2 x 5 min or 4 x 3 min loading duration.

12- to 15-year-olds

Target: From the age of 12, the differences between the sexes start to become apparent. Aerobic endurance capacity can be developed very well. Rest break length: longer than 2 min.

Exercises: 3 x 5 min or 4 x 4 min or 5 x 3 min or 6 x 2 min or 2 x 6/7 min or (in minutes) 6-5-4-3-2 or 2-3-4-5-4-3-2 loading duration.

From the age of 15

Target: The development of the cardiovascular system is maximal in 15- to 16-year-old girls. In boys, this lasts until the ages of 18 to 22. The aerobic endurance can be trained. Anaerobic loads are possible from the age of 16.

Exercises: 3 x 7 or 3 x 8 min or 3 x 10 min or (in minutes) 10-8-6-4 or 6 x 4-5 min or 5 x 5-6 min loading duration.

The Development of Speed in Talented Youngsters at 2010 Dutch Champions FC Twente Enschede

5- to 6-year-olds

Target: From the ages of 5-6, an increase is movement speed is accompanied by improved coordination. Reaction speed can be developed.

Training games: Different training games, reaction games with the emphasis on sensory motor skills: touch, sight and hearing.

7- to 9-year-olds

Target: Between the ages of 7 and 9, the basic qualities of an effective running technique improve and the number of speed exercises should be increased. Reaction ability improves from age 9 onward, and there is a significant improvement in movement frequency.

Training games: Conscious movement training by frequency training with tires and poles.

10- to 11-year-olds

Target: Movements become increasingly dynamic. Different (partial) techniques are integrated into the overall movement sequence, which can lead to an improvement in movement frequency.

Exercises: Further development of frequency by means of conscious and unconscious running training, and through drills using ladders, tires and posts.

12- to 15-year-olds

Target: Start of the optimum phase of speed development. Boys can use their strength abilities in a targeted way, thereby increasing their speed.

Exercises: Conscious training of the (partial) techniques. Introduction of running drills. Speed training, e.g., 6-8 x 10m sprints from different positions or 6m x 5m shuttle runs.

From 15 years

Target: Maximal development of speed and further increase in the differences between the sexes. Strength development in girls stabilizes and increases in boys. By improving strength, the different forms of speed can be further developed alongside the improvement in technique with the aid of targeted and conscious sprint training.

Exercises: Examples: 4 x 10m sprints or 4 x 15 m shuttle runs.

The Development of Coordination and Mobility in Talented Youngsters at 2010 Dutch Champions FC Twente Enschede

5- to 6-year-olds

Target: Mobility can be developed well. Motor learning performance increases between the ages of 5 and 6. Simple abilities and skills can be learned well.

Training Games: Lots of rhythmic exercises with diverse movements. Development of simple running, jumping and throwing.

7- to 9-year-olds

Target: Mobility increases. Basic motor skills are further developed by increasingly differentiated movement forms. Soccer-specific techniques can now be introduced.

Exercises: Build-up of technical abilities and skills using different movement arrangements in different situations.

12- to 15-year-olds

Target: First signs of stagnation in technical abilities and skills. Performance levels can be further developed using specific technique training. Absolute motor learning performance is reduced, but not for certain movement techniques that have already been mastered.

Exercises: many mobility exercises with different equipment or a partner. Repetition and intensification of the soccer-specific techniques that have already been mastered. Variations in organization forms and technique training..

From the age of 15

Target: In boys, dynamism in the execution of movement techniques increases due to the gain in strength. Mobility gradually decreases.

Training games: A varied range of exercises will ensure that technique is improved and further optimized. They create a rich variety of game and movement situations. Focus more specifically on mobility.

Conditioning training for young talents at FC Twente Enschede is also supplemented (depending on coaching and developmental levels) by individual training plans that include relaxation techniques, stabilization and balance exercises, function-related stretching programs and auxiliary equipment.

The presentation of Harry Dost's training philosophy impressed the authors by its detailed structure and clear identification of the training goals and methods in conditioning training for talented youngsters at FC Twente Enschede. If we compare Dost's conditioning training with the coaching and training philosophy of FC Twente Enschede described in Chapter 6.5, the great importance of the core skills of *coordination* and *mobility* for the desired dominance of the team when they and the opponents have the ball becomes abundantly clear. They act as a kind of link between the core sports motor skills of speed, strength and endurance, and technical and tactical abilities and skills with and without the ball. Precise and fast movement control coupled with a maximally perfect use of all degrees of motion within the musculoskeletal system are considered to be *the* prerequisites for the implementation of Dutch Champions FC Twente Enschede's playing philosophy. This ensures that the club has a coherent playing, training and coaching philosophy.

10   Talent Development at Ajax Amsterdam in Theory and Practice

> *"Totaal voetbal* [total soccer] not only helped Ajax Amsterdam become a dominant force at home (from 1966 to 1973, the club won the national championships six times and the Cup four times), but it enabled it to become the best club in Europe."   (Schulze-Marmeling, 2010, p 88)

The most successful of the Dutch traditional clubs and championship record-holders, Ajax Amsterdam, can boast a plethora of national and international titles.[19] For decades, Ajax Amsterdam has also been considered as *the* breeding ground for international soccer talent (see Leerkes, 2003, p. 56).

In the past, the coaching philosophy of the Dutch championship record-holders was considered to be exemplary, particularly by German clubs, coaches and officials:

*   "At Bayern, in the Franz-Beckenbauer Academy, we try to transfer Ajax Amsterdam to the German mentality" (Rummenigge, 1998, p 24).

*   "We in the *Bundesliga* [German national soccer league] can only learn from the model of youth schools similar to those at Ajax" (Schäfer quoted in Sports, 1996, p 1).

Originally, Ajax Amsterdam had set itself the objective of coaching talented youngsters for its own professional team. "On average, three new youth players should be included in Ajax's first team every two years" (Kormelink & Seeverens, 1998b, p 59). No other top-class European club has managed in recent decades to produce talents coached to such a high level for its own professional team and for other teams abroad (see Kormelink, Seeverens and Adriaanse, 1993, pps 3-11). Publicly, therefore, the Dutch coaching philosophy is usually equated with that of Ajax Amsterdam (see Chapter 4).

In particular, the transfer of highly talented soccer players has boomed since the Bosman Ruling. The high transfer fees and players' salaries have increasingly meant that future top players at Ajax Amsterdam are transferred to clubs in England, Italy, Spain and Germany.

---

19   AFC Ajax Amsterdam was founded on March 13, 1900, and has been Dutch champion 37 times, 14 times Dutch cup winner, 4 times Champions League winner (formerly European Cup for National Champions), 1 x UEFA Cup winner, 1 x European Cup winners Cup, 3 x European Super Cup winners and 2 x World Cup winners.

But what makes Ajax Amsterdam's playing and coaching philosophy so admired and popular and how has it changed in recent decades?

10.1 The Previous Coaching Philosophy of Ajax Amsterdam

For German youth talent expert Norbert Vieth (1995, p 31), the secret of Ajax Amsterdam's success is the "close and consistent collaboration between the youth and professional sections," whereby the professional department sets the guidelines for youth coaching. "In this way, the unique Ajax culture opens up important lines of communication between the youth, amateur and professional sections." (Hüring, 1994, p 3). Kormelink & Seeverens (1998b, p 59) indicate that between the three abovementioned sections there is an "internal communication," which actually enables it to function significantly above average. In addition, it should be noted that at Ajax Amsterdam there is collaboration in terms of content and personnel between the junior and senior sections. "After training with the pro goalkeepers, Frans Hoek enjoys only a quick break before directly going to the next pitch to work with the junior goalkeepers" (Vieth, 1995, p 31). All members of the training staff know the demand profile for professional soccer in general and the Ajax playing style in particular, and can therefore include key coaching components and innovations in the youth training program in a timely manner (see Chapters 10.2 and 10.5). The promotion of an A junior coach to head coach of the first senior team has a tradition in this club (see Kormelink & Seeverens, 2001, p 8). "The success of the youth concept is exclusively measured on how many players go on to play on the professional team" Hyballa, 2003a, p 22). For this reason, *the development of individual players* at Ajax Amsterdam is placed at the center of their coaching conception and is implemented by a coaching staff with a very low turnover. Those in charge at Ajax Amsterdam ensure continuity by virtue of the way their young, talented players are coached.

Their own playing culture is above all characterized by the urge to play offensively, which is also reflected in different coaching and playing personalities, such as Rinus Michels, Johan Cruyff and Louis van Gaal, but also by socio-cultural developments in Amsterdam and the whole country (see Winner, 2008, pps 49-67). However, it also depends on the choice of young, talented players who adapt to this particular playing culture. [20]

---

20 Statistics from the year 1998 show that the coaching system of Ajax Amsterdam used to produce 1.5 players for the Dutch national side every two years (see SID, 1998, p 13).

10.1.1 Ajax Talent

The Ajax Coaching system is responsible for about 160 talented youngsters, who are primarily selected according to four criteria:

1. Technique

2. Intelligence

3. Personality and

4. Speed (see Kormelink & Seeverens, 1998b, p 60)

At Ajax Amsterdam, these four features form the category system and analytical framework, called TIPS, for the evaluation of a talented player. The features are regularly analyzed and interpreted during the course of a season. "If someone does not fulfill the criteria, at the end of the season they must leave the club" (Leerkes, 2003, p 56). Height, strength and length and width growth are not important in the selection of talent, as they should only be worked on later in the training process, which means the talent scouts of Ajax Amsterdam concentrate primarily on players' creative and technical actions.[21]

---

21 SC Heerenveen scouts its talents according to the criteria of Speed, Technique, (Game) Intelligence and Mentality, also known as "STIM." As in the TIPS system, and in the descriptions with regard to the general Dutch talent scouting in Chapter 3, these elementary performance factors produce a permanently offensive playing style.

10.2   The Ajax Playing Style

The offensive Ajax playing style was perfectly suited to the 1-3-4-3 system (see Fig. 79) until 2001. Johan Cruyff and Louis van Gaal were the proponents of this style.

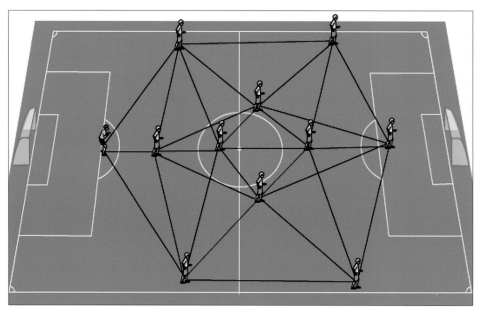

Fig. 79: The 1-3-4-3 system predominantly used by the Ajax Amsterdam youth section until 2001.

Because "the build-up phase in the overly rigid Ajax concept was too stereotypical, and a few players lacked the playing philosophy" (Kormelink & Seeverens, 2001, p. 5), the playing system was modified to a 1-4-3-3. That meant that the Ajax juniors no longer played with three defenders in a line, but with four defenders responsible for zonal defense. To this end, a midfield player had to drop back to play defensively (see Chapter 8.2). At Ajax now, they assume that four defenders playing flexibly can organize the build-up from the defense so that it is particularly easier to play a pass out to the wing. This is combined, especially when Ajax has the ball, *with creative and forward-directed play* in which the ball can be passed both inward and outward. Kormelink & Seeverens (2001, p.6) stress that four players on the back line can also be very advantageous when the opposing team has the ball. "The additional defender narrows the gaps in the team's own defensive zone thus making the team less vulnerable to counterattacks by the opposite team."

As can be seen from Chapters 6.4 and 10.5, coaching at Ajax is now much more oriented toward available "playing material" (Kormelink & Seeverens, 2002, p. 5).

The playing systems merge into each other so that the young Ajax players also learn the 1-3-4-3 system alongside the 1-4-3-3. "The system is no longer the most important thing" (ibid, 2001, p 6). Instead, the offensive playing style, i.e., the behavior of each player when in possession of the ball, is strongly emphasized in coaching. The basis of the coaching conception forms the 1-4-3-3 system in which, as a rule, the best soccer players play in the positions of center forward (9), offensive midfielder (10) and center back (4). In these positions, the results of TIC should be particularly evident and effective (see ibid). All youth coaches and teams must be guided by a coherent coaching concept (see Chapter 10.5; Kormelink, Seeverens & Adriaanse, 1993).

10.3   Ajax Training

Alongside the practically coaching emphases, young Ajax players also learn the following theoretical basics of their game:

"Technique, tactics, expertise, running and strength training, personality building, coaching moments, training and matches" (Kormelink & Seeverens, 1998b, p.64).

The youth coaches select the drills and training games for their teams, the only restriction being that they must be suitable for the youngsters' developmental stage (ibid). "The E juniors coach knows exactly what his boys must be able to do in order to move up to the D juniors" (Leerkes, 2003, p. 56). The predominant coaching principle is dictated by TIPS, so that at the start of the coaching process the focus is initially on the many different techniques, and is followed by a smooth transition into the area of tactical abilities and skills.

In every training session, Ajax coaches integrate the technical abilities and skills into the warm-up phase and they are constantly solicited right up to the professional level. "Passing and shooting on goal are the foundation of a soccer player" (Smink, 2002, p. 20). As can be deduced from Chapter 8.4.1, training games for the different team positions and small-sided games constitute other, constantly recurring emphases of a training session. The training games and small-sided games are intensively coached by Ajax trainers. That is a particular feature of the training work at Ajax Amsterdam. This includes *task-oriented* coaching on the part of the Ajax trainers, who set (1) tactical and/or (2) communicative tasks (see also Chapter 5.2).

- Examples of (1): stopping game situations combined with a brief and targeted instruction, which should optimize the players' future match behavior (variation: introduction of provocation rules).

- Examples of (2): short, sharp and clear code words for certain game situations (player-coach, coach-player, player-player).

This constantly recurring sequence within the training sessions is supplemented by individual training programs (e.g., running coordination, goalkeeping training and testing/measuring).

Finally, the typical Ajax training can be summed up by the following quotes:

- "A training session must always have a goal: it must be very work-intensive and attractive for the players" (Kormelink & Seeverens, 1998b, p 70).

- One "can learn a great deal of training drills by rote but much more important is the ability to intervene at the right time, make the right analysis and to show how something is done" (ibid).

10.4   Ajax Coaching Staff

Ajax Amsterdam places high demands on both its players and coaches (see Chapter 10.5).

As well as the presence and/or acquisition of the highest coaching licenses in the KNVB, Kormelink, Seeverens and Danny Blind single out the following typical features of an Ajax coach:

- Every "youth coach must be 'happy' with his position and be clear that his job is very important" (Kormelink & Seeverens, 1998b, p. 70).

- The coaches should always structure their training from the perspective of the playing system, thus enabling a smooth transition from age group to age group.

- The F to D junior coaches must be young and able to understand where their players are coming from. However, the A junior coaches must have very good tactical training and be able to explain tactical measures clearly (see ibid).

- The coaches must work constantly to increase their knowledge.

- "The coaches in the youth section at Ajax Amsterdam must have a message that is understood and put into practice by the players" (Blind, 8.5.2003).

10.5   The New Ajax Model:
Heroes of the Future

In 2007, masterminded by Wim Zielhorst and Maarten Stekelenburg in collaboration with Armada Sports and AFC Ajax Amsterdam, six DVDs appeared under the title *Heroes of the Future*, which present a summary of the theory and practice of *Ajax Education* for the age groups 7-12, 12-15 and 15-18.

The first part of *Ajax Education* deals with "the Ajax playing style" and is explained below in the form of a summary of a description of the contents.

- The "Club" Ajax Amsterdam decides the playing style of the teams, not the coaches, whereby Ranolds and Michels are considered to be the first developers of the offensive playing style at Ajax Amsterdam.

- *The Ajax Playing Style* can be characterized by three features: technical play, attacking and entertainment.

- The young talents at Ajax Amsterdam are characterized by their mastery of two performance components:
  1. Technique.
  2. Tactics (what do I do from my position?).

- *Playing system:* After the age of 10, the 1-4-3-3 and 1-3-4-3 (11 players) formations can be played. Prior to this, in training and matches, the young Ajax Amsterdam talents play 1-3-3 (seven players), 1-3-1-3 (eight players) and 1-3-2-3 systems (nine players). At senior level, the playing systems 1-3-4-3 and 1-4-4-2 are traditionally linked to the trademark of Ajax Amsterdam, combination play.

- The *playing concept* consists of four features:
  1. Helping each other.
  2. The central defender also pushes forward.
  3. In the opponent's half, 1-on-1 situations should be deliberately sought.
  4. In 1-on-1 situations look for chances to score.

- *Possession of the ball and pitch mastery:* Ball possession is key to pitch mastery and is characterized by
  a. Fast ball circulation (ideally with one-touch combinations).
  b. A passing and dribbling speed that is adapted to the teammates.
  c. A clear passing direction (as a foundation of positional play).
  d. Security.
  e. Timely situation anticipation and coordination relating to all positions within a team (in particular, play off the ball).

- *Opposing team's possession of the ball:* The Ajax Amsterdam youngsters should follow the principles below:
  a. Reduce the distance to the opponent.
  b. Keep the pitch small.
  c. Think about which opportunities the opponent has when in possession of the ball.
  d. Put pressure (pressing) on the teammates (individually and/or as a group).

- *Perception (orientation) and anticipation* hold special value in the playing style of Ajax Amsterdam:
  1. Choose your optimal position.
  2. When can you transfer possession of the ball?
  3. What happens after losing possession of the ball?
  4. Take an overview of the situation, make a decision and go for it!

- *Technical skills:* The technique and "visions" of the players determine the correct decision ("Make the right decision!").

- *Individual Playing style:* At Ajax Amsterdam, that means that the concept for the game is based on the players' technical qualities, and they should then act situation-appropriately and with variety and creativity.

The second part of the *Ajax Education* deals with the playing philosophy that lies behind the training concept. Under the heading "The Ajax Training Concept," a few features are outlined below:

- *Talent spotting:* Ajax coaches are particularly interested in the following performance factors: technique, reading the game (tactics), speed and discipline, self-confidence and the will to win. Therefore, particular attention is given to the individual state of development: what is special about each player? At the same time, *the* abilities and skills that players *must* be able to perform in the future in the positions on the pitch are as it were "thought ahead" by Ajax coaches. This almost inevitably influences *talent development* at Ajax: what does the player need in order to be able to cope with the training of a professional soccer player?

- *Talent Development:* On the basis of the abovementioned demands and individual features of the players, this should be particularly and intensively coached in specific developmental phases:
  1. Technique: ages 8-12.
  2. Tactics: ages 12-18.
  3. Physique: ongoing.
  4. Mental: ongoing.

This classification is reflected by Ajax Amsterdam in the formation of *three developmental stages* in training:

1st **stage** ages 8-11: positional play, technique

2nd **stage** ages 12-14: team play

3rd **stage** ages 15-18: team tactics and learning to win

These stages therefore reflect the playing philosophy, along with mental and physical developmental processes. Ajax Amsterdam places particular value on the development of every player's self-confidence. The fostering of this quality should be achieved through targeted feedback.

10.5.1 Ajax 2010: The Interview

Written interview with Olde Riekerink (Youth Talent Coordinator at Ajax Amsterdam) from March 17, 2010 (see also Chapter 6.4).

Authors: *What was Ajax Amsterdam's playing philosophy in 2010?*

OR: At Ajax, we have been working according to a specific playing philosophy for a couple of years. The strategy is that we can play out goal chances via a skilled game opening via the inside backs! This means that the outside players, the deep striker and the offensive midfielders have key roles. Ajax always tries to play in the opponents' half (pressing), for which high ball circulation and good positional play are essential. If ball possession is lost, the opponent is again put directly under pressure in order to immediately start a new game build-up.

Authors: *How often does each junior team train at Ajax Amsterdam?*

OR:

- U19 & U18 train 6 x per week.
- U17 & U16 train 5 x per week.
- U15 & U14 train 4 x per week.
- U13 & U12 train 3 x per week.
- U11 & U10 train 2 x per week.

At the moment, we are discussing whether they should train more often.

Authors: *What do you currently emphasize in Ajax youth development coaching?*

OR: In the junior section at Ajax, we develop the players very precisely and very individually. Emphasis is placed on technical abilities, tactical abilities, mental abilities and physical abilities. Using a personal development plan and video systems, we try to encourage players to achieve peak performances. We emphasize the players' individual development. We are increasingly looking at the players' individual strengths and weaknesses, and trying to improve and optimize them through a planned process.

Authors: *Which playing system do you favor in youth coaching at Ajax Amsterdam?*

OR: All Ajax junior teams use the same playing system: 1-4-3-3. Within this system, the coach may also switch between an offensive or defensive 1-3-4-3. The playing philosophy (see the answer to the first question) always remains the same and is not changeable.

Authors: *How would you characterize the playing philosophy of the Ajax junior teams?*

OR: With possession of the ball, the emphasis is on positional play with quick ball circulation during which it is important that the players aim for a certain depth on the pitch. The game mostly takes place in the opponent's half. If possession is lost, each player switches immediately, thus placing the opponent under pressure in order to regain ball possession immediately.

Authors: *According to which criteria do you assess your Ajax coaches?*

OR: Coaches are assessed according to the following criteria: they must adapt to the culture of the club and have a comprehensive knowledge of the Ajax playing style. Their pedagogical qualities and age must be appropriate for the developmental stage of their players. Above all, they must be able to work in a team!

10.5.2 The 7-12 Age Group

Irrespective of whether the ages may differ in the establishment of developmental stages and levels (see Chapter 10.5), in the new Ajax model, *Heroes of the Future*, emphases are set for the age group 7-12. They are listed below.

- The consideration of age-specific characteristics.
- Mental developmental stage.
- Motor developmental stage.
- Talent scouting.
- Technique learning and ball school.
- Technique training.
- Choice of position.
- Tactics training.
- Support and leveling.
- Playing on a team with older players.

10.5.3 The 12-15 Age Group

The new Ajax model sets the following coaching emphases for this age group:

- Consideration of age-specific characteristics (including the growth spurt).
- Passing and receiving.
- Application of technical abilities and skills.
- Positional play
- Special abilities and skills.
- Match play.

The coaching emphasizes passing, receiving and positional play, which are practiced in the following training drills with this age group at Ajax Amsterdam (see also Chapters 7.3, 8.4.2 and 8.4.3).

Fig. 80: Example of the Ajax Model passing and receiving (ibid, 2007, part 4)

Procedure

- Passing from positions 4, 5 or 6/double 6 to 7 and 8, who run into a space and are passed to, turn out ("open up") and pass to 9 and 10, who previously move in and turn in the passing direction, let the ball rebound to 7 or 8 ("move on") and then shoot on goal.
- All players except 9 and 10 then move round one position (circuit).

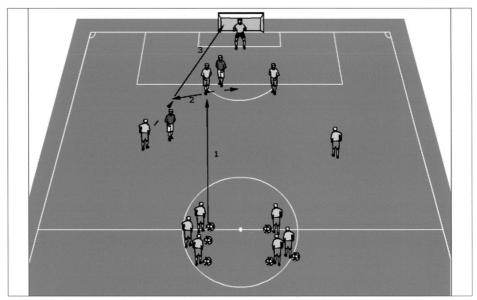

Fig. 81 (see Fig. 80): Variation with stab pass (long ball) to 9 or 10 including two opponents (ibid, 2007, part 4).

Procedure

- See Fig. 80.

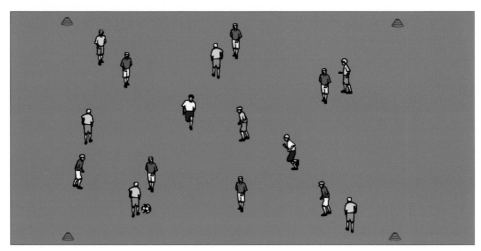

Fig. 82: Example for the Ajax model positional play: 7v7 plus two neutral players (ibid, 2007, part 4).

Procedure

- Use *training emphasis technique coaching* (bilateral passing and rebounds).

Fig. 83: Example for the Ajax model positional play: 8v6 (ibid, 2007, part 4)

Procedure

- The *training emphasis "good pitch coverage"* (use uneven-sided games or 3-2-3 system).

10.5.4 The 15-18 Age Group

In this age group, the new Ajax model contains the following coaching emphases:

- Consideration of age-specific characteristics.

- Individual playing.

- Further technical development, particularly in the areas of passing and receiving.

- Positional play.

- Team tactics.

- Match play.

- Playing concept in relation to the tactical organization of the opposite team.

The new Ajax model sets the following objectives in the *technical development* of its 15- to 18-year-olds:

- Optimization of techniques with regard to appropriate ball speed and direction.
- Quick ball speed.
- Passing to "the correct foot" (pass selection).
- High action speed.
- Initiative on the ball.
- Mutual coaching.

These objectives are followed at Ajax using the training drills below:

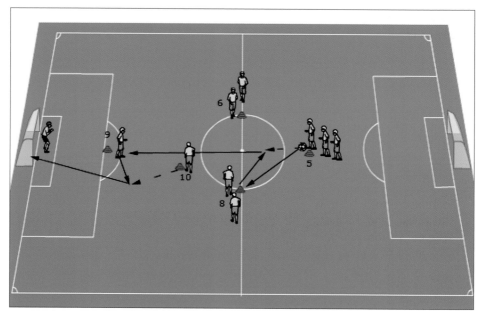

Fig. 84: Ajax model for passing and receiving for the 15-18 age group (ibid, 2007, part 5).

Procedure

- Emphasis: precise lob passing over two lines with rebound and shot on goal.
- Passing from 5 to 8, 8 lets the ball rebound and 5 plays a lob pass to 9 (in the 1-4-3-3 system), 9 lets the ball rebound to 10, who then shoots on goal.

Variations

- Involvement of positions 7 and 11 and wing play and heading.

In the area of *positional play*, the new Ajax model pursues the following objectives in training:

- Adopt position.

- Make the right decisions.

- Every pass is important.

- High ball speed.

- Frequent running movements.

- Positional play ends in a 1 on 1 with a chance to score.

In the new Ajax model, this area is very closely linked to concrete objectives for the coaching of *team tactics*:

- Learning to transfer structures and playing systems on the run with and without the ball.

- Type of teamwork.

- Variations in the switching phases.

- Knowing and transferring current playing systems (see Figs. 84, 85 and 86, and Chapter 10.2).

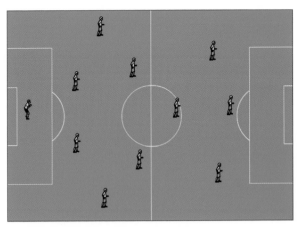

Fig. 85: Playing system 1-4-2-1-3

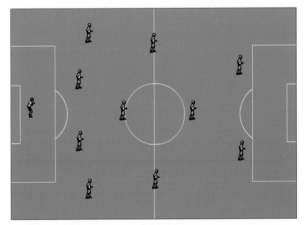

Fig. 86: Playing system 1-4-4-2

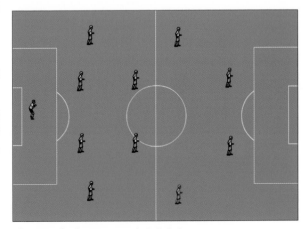

Fig. 87: Playing system 1-4-2-2-2

11 Conclusion and Outlook

"The big difference between 4-4-2 and 4-3-3 lies in the variability of the three lines (defense, midfield, forward). If you play a 4-4-2, you have four men at the back and four men in the middle, plus the two forwards, making a total of three lines. But if you play the 4-3-3 well, every five or six meters you can include extra lines, but you must know how."

(Johan Cruyff, quoted in Winner, 2008, p 355)

Vs.

"Learning and playing to win are two different things."

(Foppe de Haan, ibid)

The above two quotes show that in the Netherlands there is a lot of controversial discussion about soccer in the past, present and future. The discussions usually involve:

- The playing development of the Dutch national team in the first decade of the new century and the tension between playing attractive or results-oriented soccer.

- The partial renunciation of the Dutch 1-4-3-3 system at many senior teams in the Dutch national league.

- Johan Cruyff, often called a genius, who both as a player and coach "is the incarnation of" a "vision of harmony on the pitch" (Winner, 2008, p 360).

Events at the **2010 Soccer World Cup in South Africa** illustrate the topics discussed in the Netherlands and internationally. The Dutch national team was **World Cup runner up** and demonstrated during the tournament, among other things, many group and team tactical measures, which usually *at first glance* did not appear to fit the Dutch playing philosophy. However, as this book shows, the forms of game-opening demonstrated in the 2010 World Cup final against Spain (see 8.4.5), "ball-oriented pressing" (see Chapter 8.4.2), blocking, fast switching after winning the ball, followed by a fast attack (see Chapters 8.4.1, 8.4.3 and 8.4.6) at *second glance* are typical forms of Dutch youth coaching.

The choice of subject matter, the limited publication framework and the initial objective of this first publication on Dutch youth soccer mean that the ongoing discussions in previous chapters cannot be explained or evaluated more closely here. However, they should not be hidden. At this point, it must be stressed that the authors study the 1-4-3-3 and 1-4-4-2 playing systems very closely and learned to use and play them both as coaches and players, and as German coaches and players at that, with German soccer coaching licenses in German leagues. Their great respect and admiration for the achievements of Dutch soccer as a whole makes it almost impossible for them to actively participate in this ongoing discussion process around the "identity of Dutch soccer in the 21st century." However, they do attempt to do this from a neutral position with regard to content and methodology.

The authors strive to show that youth development coaching in the Netherlands cannot be represented as a monolithic block.

In Chapters 3.2, 4, 6, 9 and 10 it is clear that the innovative and forward-thinking Dutch national team coaches Henk Kesler and Rinus Michels who initiated a "coaching offensive" for future and already qualified trainers, referees and officials, intended to give every youngster in the Netherlands access to well-founded soccer coaching. Currently, around 2,600 amateur clubs in the Netherlands form the foundation for 16 regional specialist schools of the professional clubs. The connection between the clubs and the association KNVB (see Chapter 5.1) was created to prevent gaps arising between the grassroots level and the top level. "Everyone knows that the individual player is the most important thing – both in the professional and amateur clubs" (Reynierse quoted in Bertram, 2010, p 117). Structures are important, but they do not produce spirit. This spirit is internationally linked with *myth, philosophy, vision and process*. But what do these terms really say about the Dutch spirit in soccer? *All talented youth players in the Netherlands are permanently engaged in training and matches in the game build-up and in offensive and defensive play*. This objective is very demanding, and requires well-trained coaches and time to be performed well in matches (see Michels, 2000b): the 0:2 defeat of FC Bayern Munich in the Champions League final against Inter Milan on May 22 2010 in Madrid illustrates this Dutch philosophy of soccer. With about 65% of the ball possession in the whole game and a dominance in the opponent's half, the team was not able to convert this offensive way of playing into a victory. However, soccer coach[22] Louis van Gaal and his players remained true to this philosophy during the whole match and, undeterred, showed the fans/spectators a very committed, attractive and offensive game. The opponents, on the other hand, played strongly and deliberately with a "blanket defense" with a goalkeeper who had an outstanding match.

---

22   Soccer coach always includes the Dutch job title, Coaches Betaald Voetbal.

This defensive game allowed the Inter Milan team to frequently defend in a corridor of at most 40m x 60m, whereas van Gaal's team, with its offensive game, had to play on and defend around 90m x 60m. It is obvious that *quantitatively*, the degree of difficulty in the playing philosophy of coach van Gaal can be judged to be very high. Qualitatively, the offensive approach of the Dutch coach ensures an exciting match, because due to the size of the pitch, depending on the players' performance level, there is a constant switch between offensive and defensive play.

The KNVB assumes the role of "ideas provider" in Dutch youth soccer (Visionary [see Chapter 6.1]) and searcher/striver (philosopher) of the best coaching for talented young players. It offers the clubs, interested parties, coaches, officials, players and parents a "total vision of youth soccer," which was transferred into a "youth soccer master plan" in 2010. The key measurement tool in the learning process of young Dutch soccer players is therefore the game itself. "Everything starts and finishes with the game, which is where you show what you can do.

Physique, technique, strategy: everything belongs together and must be trained together in order to be used to advantage in a match" (Reynierse quoted in Bertram, 2010, p 114). The game represents a kind of test situation: what can the player do and what stops him from playing well? Considered in this way, the path to an optimal game represents a "soccer learning process" (see KNVB, 2001, p 2). The individual elements that constitute the game are included in the TIC model: technique, (game) intelligence and communication. However, is this model also effective in the 21st century? In the future, will it also train enough players for all performance levels in the Netherlands? The Zeist Vision of the KNVB provides an answer to this: Dutch youth development coaching is set up to ensure playing enjoyment and performance optimization (see Chapter 6.1), competitive forms of street soccer, small-sided games, positional play games involving team-oriented communication. In this way, both the development of young players at both the grassroots level (mass and leisure sport) and the elite level (talent development) are addressed. In the terminology of kinetics/kinesiology, this intrinsic "training methodology" (see Chapter 6.1.1) is referred to as an *implicit* process. This means a learning process that is highly complex and non-standardized that should be initiated by means of methodical game series (see Roth, 2005, p 300). The methodical procedure places particular demands on the coach who, in the Netherlands, acts as *coach, advisor, mentor and supporter of the young players* (see Chapter 5.2).

Implicit learning is at odds with training philosophies (see Chapter 6) that choose communication models that are geared to the coaching of automatic actions by constant repetition and correction of isolated technical-tactical features in youth coaching (see also Chapter 7.3 and 7.4). However, it can happen that, in particular at youth development level, Dutch national league clubs use a hybrid of *implicit and explicit learning processes* (via methodical series) in training. The low complexity and high standardization of *explicit learning processes* is driven by methodical exercise and situation series in youth development training (see Chapters 7.5 and 10).

If we also consider the adjectives used to frequently describe Dutch soccer, such as *total* ("totalvoetbal" [total soccer]), *offensive and dominant*, as ways of measuring the coaching of technical, tactical, conditioning, mental and communicative performance components, we can note the following:

> A talented young Dutch player should demonstrate a willingness to perform, take the initiative in the game, use his dominance in positional play and where conditioning is concerned, be capable of combining a willingness to run with fast playing pace.

The KNVB and many Dutch coaches in professional soccer agree that young players should be coached in the context of *integrated coaching* for the first senior team, and that winning should play a subordinate role in the training process (see Chapter 3.3).

One can characterize the coaching philosophy of the association and clubs as *perspective-oriented, long-term and experience-oriented*. The optimization of the performance component technique is the focus of Dutch youth development coaching because all participants believe this leads to attractive and technique-oriented soccer in matches (see Chapter 7). At this point, a clear difference between the objectives in junior and senior soccer is made (see the opening quote by Foppe de Haan). The pressure of "having to win" makes way for the perspective-oriented coaching that uses a development-oriented phase model (see Chapters 4.5 and 10.5) designed with the future in mind. The Ajax model, *Heroes of the Future*, also clearly demonstrates this classification impressively on the level of coaching in the clubs of the national league: De *toekomst* (The Future) is the name of the Ajax training academy.

In regards to content, the focus is on offensive soccer based on individual coaching with the emphasis on the 1 on 1 that aims for creativity, positional play, ball possession, the "creation" of scoring chances, communication and the optimal field coverage in a playing system with three strikers. This genuinely deductive approach is in the Netherlands also applied to conditioning training (see Chapter 9) and goalkeeping training (see Chapter 7.5):

> Everything begins and ends with the game.

Dr. Raymond Verheijen and Guus Hinink are responsible for the intensive discussions now taking place among experts on soccer conditioning. In the Olympics, this has already been carried out for many years (see Chapters 9.2.1 and 9.2.2). Further empirical studies would be desirable as the didactics and methodology of the Dutch version of soccer conditioning, which *a priori* is carried out at senior level, could have great implications for the training structure in the youth development coaching in other countries.

If we follow the most recent comments of the coaches of the Dutch soccer academy, the basic policy is not dogmatic when it comes to *aavallend voetbal* (offensive soccer) (see Reynierse quoted after Bertram, 2010, p 114). This can be reasoned as follows:

> From a didactic point of view, the coaching of young talents in the Netherlands in the four main phases of tactics training represents the common ground on which the game is structured (see Chapter 8.3).

It is understandable that an integrative coaching system must set rules, courses and regulations in order to be able to offer about 600 seminars with the abovementioned objectives. At the same time though, it also faces different expectations from coaches who want more individual freedoms in the development of their own coaching work and peripheral (also external) coaching offers (see Chapters 7.3 and 7.4).

Currently, about 125 coaches are working with a Dutch professional license outside their country of birth: Louis van Gaal, Huub Stevens, Guus Hiddink (since summer 2010 Turkish national coach), René Meulensteen (First Team Coach Manchester United), Ricardo Moins (Assistant Coach, Red Bull Salzburg), Tom Sandfiet (Namibian national coach), Co Adriaanse (Head Coach of the Qatar Olympic team), Han Berger (Technical Director at the Australian Soccer Association), Foppe de Haan (Coach at Ajax Cape Town), etc. Why is this? "We are used to adapting to other cultures and countries, and we quickly learn foreign languages so that we can fit in anywhere" (Marsman quoted after Bertram, 2010, p 112; see te Poel, 2002, pps 46-49). The Dutch magazine

SoccerCoaching-International highlights the international orientation of Dutch soccer experts. It appears in the Netherlands in English six times per year and is now also distributed online

If we ask Dennis Bergkamp, who is mentioned by many Dutch people in the same breath as "soccer greats" Marco van Basten and Johan Cruyff, whether there is a distinctive Dutch playing style that is now also practiced worldwide by coaches of other nationalities and can be integrated into existing coaching systems without friction, the former national striker and player at Arsenal (London) and Ajax Amsterdam answers with a reference to a vision of creative, attacking soccer that does not lose sight of the result of the match (see Bergkamp, quoted in Winner, 2010, p 93; McShane, 2002).

Does that mean that soccer training in the Dutch coaching system, which is characterized by the vision of an attractive and offensive soccer game on a global scale actually enables internationalism and integration?

Additional qualitative and quantitative research is required in order to make general statements about:

- Actual coaching content and methods in the micro, macro, meso, annual and multi-year cycles in Dutch clubs and the KNVB
- The pedagogical methods.
- The socio-cultural characteristics of the Dutch vision of soccer.

12 Appendix

Electronic Media

Ajax Amsterdam. (1996). *Koordinationstraining. Physische Aspekte. Die Ajax-Schule Teil 1.* Hengelo: Sport Video Productions.

Coerver, W. (no year). *COERVER Fundamentals. Part three. Heading and shooting.* Reedswain.

Dusseldorp, W., Kormelink, H., Seeverens, T. & Vergoossen, S. (2001). *Die eigene Technik verbessern. Die niederländische Fußballschule Teil 7.* Leer: Bfp Versand Anton Lindemann.

Dusseldorp, W., Seeverens, T. & Vergoossen, S. (2000). *Verteidigen von 11:11 zu 1:1. Die niederländische Fußballschule Teil 3.* Leer: Bfp Versand Anton Lindemann.

Dusseldorp, W., Seeverens, T. & Vergoossen, S. (2001). *Das 4-3-3-System. Die niederländische Fußballschule Teil 5.* Leer: Bfp Versand Anton Lindemann.

Dost, H. (no year). *Voetbal looptechnik.* Hengelo.

Galustian, A. & Cooke, C. (1998). *Coerver® Coaching video. Building essential skills. Masterclass Series Part Two.* Cincinnati: Sportsmethod Ltd.

Galustian, A. & Cooke, C. (2005). *Coerver® Coaching. Make your move. Part 3: Adding to skills.* Reedswain.

Galustian, A. & Cooke, C. (2008a). *Coerver® Coaching. Improve your game. Part 1: Skills.* Center Circle Produktions, LLC.

Galustian, A. & Cooke, C. (2008b). *Coerver® Coaching. Super skills.* Center Circle Produktions, LLC.

Hoek, F. (no year). *Der Fußball Torwart. Teil 1.* HA Hoorn.

Hoek, F. (no year). *Der Fußball Torwart. Teil 2.* HA Hoorn.

Michels, R. & Vergoossen, S. (2001). *Vom Straßenfußball zum Wettkampf. Der Lernprozess im Fußball. Die niederländische Fußballschule. Teil 8.* Leer: Bfp Versand Anton Lindemann.

Schreiner, P. & Thissen, G. (2008). *Koordinationstraining Fußball. GLEICHGEWICHT. Der Schlüssel zur Perfektion am Ball.* o. O.

Zielhorst, W. & Stekelenburg, M. (2007). *HEROES OF THE FUTURE. The Ajax education. Part 1 to Part 6.* Reedswain.

Bibliography

Barend, F. & van Dorp, H. (2006). *Ajax-Barcelona-Cruijff. Das ABC eines eigensinnigen Maestros.* München: Bombus.

Barez, A. (2010). Vom Großen Fußball lernen! *fußballtraining, 6+7,* 40-53.

Bayer 04 Leverkusen. (2000). *Informationen zum Juniorenkonzept von Bayer 04 Leverkusen.* Leverkusen: Bayer 04 Leverkusen.

Bertram, J. (2010). Der Geist von Zeist. *11 Freunde, 11* (#102), 110-117.

Biermann, C. & Fuchs, U. (1999). *Der Ball ist rund, damit das Spiel die Richtung ändern kann. Wie moderner Fußball funktioniert.* Köln: Kiepenheuer & Witsch.

Bisanz, G. & Vieth, N. (2000). *Fußball von morgen. Teil 2. Leistungstraining für B-/A-Junioren und Amateure.* Münster: Philippka-Sportverlag.

Bode, G. (2001). F- und E-Junioren-Training. *fußballtraining, 5+6,* 26-31.

Boesten, E. (no year). *Sport in Holland. Wie man in Nijmegen deutsche Jugendfußballer scoutet.* Zugriff am 18. März 2003 unter www.holland-news.de/themen/sport/anekdoten/anek3.htm.

Boudeweel, T. (2002). „Bij zonevoetbal gaat het om het permanente evenwicht". *De Voetbaltrainer, 110,* 12-17.

Broich, H., Brauch, S. & Mester, J. (2008). Evaluierung der Laufdistanzen in unterschiedlichen Geschwindigkeitsbereichen im Profifußball. *Leistungssport, 38* (4), 8-12.

Brüggemann, D. (2000). Jugendfußball – der Zankapfel der Nation. *fußballtraining, 11+12,* 58-65.

Coenen, J. (1998). Rudi Völler „Die Nationalelf hat uns den UEFA-Cup gekostet". *Sport-Bild, 46,* 35.

Coerver, W. & Galustian, A. (1995). *SCORE! Soccer tactics & techniques for a better offensive.* New York: Sterling Publishing Co.

Cruijff, J. (2002). *Ik houd van voetbal.* 's-Gravenhage: BZZZToh bv.

De Voetbaltrainer. (2000). Teambuilding als route naar succes. De meest complete „voetbalbijbel". *De Voetbaltrainer, 87,* 7-11.

de Vries, M. & van Rossum, J. (1998). *Talentontwikkeling. Tactisch inzicht.* Arnhem: NOC+NSF.

Den Otter, P. (2002). Geen enkele visie is heilig. *De Voetbaltrainer, 104*, 51-53.

Dollemann, G. (1998). *Interval Sprint & Interval Shuttle Run Test.* Abschlussarbeit des Instituts für Bewegungswissenschaften. Rijksuniversität Groningen.

Dost, H. (no year). *Werkboek fysieke training in jeugdvoetbal.* Een praktische benadering. o. O.

Dost, H. (2003). *Koordination im Fußball.* IFKT-Workshop Duisburg-Wedau vom 30. März 2003. o. O.

Ferguson, A. (2000). *Managing my life.* London.

Flick, U. (1999). *Qualitative Forschung. Theorie, Methoden, Anwendung in Psychologie und Sozialwissenschaften.* Reinbek: Rowohlt.

Galustian, A. & Cooke, C. (1998). *A Coerver® Coaching masterclass series.* Cincinnati: Sportsmethod Ltd.

Galustian, A. & Wieczorek, R. (2010). Coerver® Coaching: Über individuelle Klasse zum Erfolg. Warum nur Talente mit perfekten Basistechniken große Karrieren machen. *fußballtraining, 5,* 30-39.

Geurts, S. (1999). „Winnen moet, maar voetballen is veel meer . . .". *De Voetbaltrainer, 81,* 33-37.

Hägele, M. (1996). Tore und Tränen. *Sports, 4,* 48-54.

Hägele, M., Wahl, P., Sperlich, B. & Mester, J. (2009). Aktiv oder passiv – der Effekt unterschiedlicher Erholungsprotokolle nach hochintensivem Intervall-Training (HIT). *Leistungssport, 39* (6), 10-14.

Hebestreit, H., Mimura, K.I. & Bar-Or, O. (1993). Recovery of muscle power after high-intensity short-term exercise: comparing boys and men. *J. Appl. Physiol., 74,* 2875-2880.

Heflik, A. (1997). Van Cruijff tot Klinsmann. De bewegen geschiednis van twee voetbalnaties. In R. Slotboom (Red.), *Nederland – Duitsland,* S. 38-45. Utrecht / Antwerpen: Kosmos-Z&K Uitgevers.

Helgerud, J., Hoydal, K., Wang, E., Karlsen, T. & Berg, P. (2007). Aerobic high intensity intervals improve VO_2max more than moderate training. *Med. Sci. Ecerc., 39* (4), 665-671.

Hohmann, A. (2001). Leistungsdiagostische Kriterien sportlichen Talents. *Leistungssport, 31,* 14-22.

Hohmann, A., Kolb, M. & Roth, K. (Hrsg.). (2005). *Handbuch Sportspiel.* Schorndorf: Hofmann.

Hoek, F. (1990). *Torwarttraining.* München: BLV.

Hof, M. (2001). Sterk aan de bal. *De Voetbaltrainer, 98,* 52-57.

Hoff, J., Kähler, N. & Helgerud, J. (2006). Training sowie Ausdauer und Krafttests von professionellen Fußball-Spielern. *Deutsche Zeitschrift für Sportmedizin, 57* (5), 116-124.

Hofmann, S. & Schneider, G. (1985). Eingangsbeurteilung und Auswahl im Nachwuchsleistungssport. *Theorie und Praxis der Körperkultur, 34,* 44-52.

Hottenrott, H. & Neumann, G. (2010). Ist das Superkompensationsmodell noch aktuell? *Leistungssport, 40* (2), 13-19.

Hübner, R. (2000). *Traumziel FC Bayern. Vom Talent zum Profi.* München: BLV.

Hüring, H. (1994). Fußball international: Ajax Amsterdam. *fußballtraining, 7,* 3-23.

Hubers, P. (2000). Onderzoek naar jeugdopleiding in Nederland. *De Voetbaltrainer, 87,* 48-61.

Hyballa, P. (1999). Was ist das Erfolgsrezept der niederländischen Talentförderung? *fußballtraining, 8,* 4-14.

Hyballa, P. (2000). Leichtfüßig agieren – erfolgreicher spielen! Teil 1. *fußballtraining, 7,* 36-41.

Hyballa, P. (2001a). B- und A-Junioren-Training. *fußballtraining, 5 + 6,* 40-47.

Hyballa, P. (2001b). Bei Turnieren sind alle Sieger! *fußballtraining, 4,* 6-13

Hyballa, P. (2001c). Talent promotion: What's the secret of Holland's success? *Success in soccer, 1,* 4-13.

Hyballa, P. (2001d). Wir soll(t)en miteinander reden! *fußballtraining, 11 + 12,* 42-45.

Hyballa, P. (2002a). Gesucht wird: der dritte Mann. *fußballtraining, 11 + 12,* 52-57.

Hyballa, P. (2002b). Mit dem Pass in die Tiefe nach oben. *fußballtraining, 8,* 32-37.

Hyballa, P. (2003a). Es STIMmt beim SC Heerenveen. *fußballtraining, 7,* 16-21.

Hyballa, P. (2003b). Der Einzelspieler ist wichtiger als das System. *fußballtraining, 8,* 22-27.

Hyballa, P. & te Poel, H.-D. (2009). Wenn das Fußballtalent im Mathematikunterricht an den Doppelpass denkt. Wechselwirkungen zwischen Schule und Fußball im Leben eines zukünftigen Nationalspielers. In R. Naul & U. Wick (Hrsg.), *20 Jahre dvs-Kommission Fußball. Herausforderung für den Fußballsport in Schule und Verein* (S. 99-111). Hamburg: Czwalina.

Job, B. (2010). Der Geist von Zeist. *11 Freunde, 11* (#102), 110-117.

Joch, W. (1992). *Das sportliche Talent.* Aachen: Meyer & Meyer.

Kluge, F. (1999). *Etymologisches Wörterbuch der deutschen Sprache.* Berlin.

KNVB. (1996). *Het Jeugdplan Nederland – Leidraad voor het jeugdvoetballeerproces en talentontwikkeling.* Zeist: KNVB.

KNVB. (2001). Masterplan Jeugdvoetbal. Zeist: KNVB.

KNVB. (2010). *Wettspielsystem.* Zugriff am 20. April 2010 unter www.knvb.nl

KNVB Academie. (2000). *KNVB – jeugdvoetbal – talentontwikkeling.* Zeist: KNVB.

KNVB Academie. (2002). *Brochure opleidingen.* Zeist: KNVB.

KNVB Academie. (2010a). *Inhalte Kursangebote F- bis D-Pupillen.* Zugriff am 26. April 2010 unter www.academie.knvb.nl/cursusInfo/

KNVB Academie. (2010b). *Internationale Projekte.* Zugriff am 20. April 2010 unter www.academie.knvb.nl/index.cfm?fuseaction=international.start&CFID=1331611 &CFTOKEN =34821147

KNVB Academie. (2010c). *Ausbildungsprogramm.* Zugriff am 25. April 2010 unter www.academie.knvb.nl/index.cfm

KNVB Academie. (2010d). *Online Bibliothek.* Zugriff am 22. April 2010 unter www.sportlink.com/manager/dms/index.php?option=com_content&view= article&id=21

KNVB Academie. (2010e). *Niederländischer Juniorenfußball.* Zugriff am 24. April 2010 unter www.junioren.voetbal.nl/

Kormelink, H. (1999). Er is wel genoeg talent in Nederland! *De Voetbaltrainer, 81,* 8-18.

Kormelink, H. (2000). „Du mußt ein talentierter Trainer sein, um mit Talenten zu arbeiten!" *fußballtraining, 11 + 12,* 69-73.

Kormelink, H. (2001a). Masterplan bepalend voor toekomst Nederlands voetbal? *De Voetbaltrainer, 100,* 29-33.

Kormelink, H. (2001b). Regiocoaches aan de basis. *De Voetbaltrainer, 95,* 30-32.

Kormelink, H. (2002). Training talent the Dutch way. *Success in Soccer, 5,* 34-37.

Kormelink, H. & Pabst, K. (2002). Das Umschalten effektiv trainieren. *fußballtraining, 10,* 26-31.

Kormelink, H. & Seeverens, T. (1998a). De Coerver-plus methode. *De Voetbaltrainer, 76,* 20-29.

Kormelink, H. & Seeverens, T. (1998b). *Die Trainingsphilosophie von Louis van Gaal und den Ajax-Trainern.* Leer: Bfp Versand Anton Lindemann.

Kormelink, H. & Seeverens, T. (1999a). Een training begint bij de eindvorm! *De Voetbaltrainer, 85,* 2-13.

Kormelink, H. & Seeverens, T. (1999b). *Jugendfußball in den Niederlanden.* Leer: Bfp Versand Anton Lindemann.

Kormelink, H. & Seeverens, T. (1999c). „Stap voor stap naar het ideale oranje". *De Voetbaltrainer, 80,* 2-13.

Kormelink, H. & Seeverens, T. (1999d). Talentontwikkeling: een zeer complexe materie. *De Voetbaltrainer, 81,* 2-7.

Kormelink, H. & Seeverens, T. (1999e). Trainen vanuit een spelconcept. *De Voetbaltrainer, 85,* 40-45.

Kormelink, H. & Seeverens, T. (2000). *Wettkampfanalyse und Spielvorbereitung.* Leer: Bfp Versand Anton Lindemann.

Kormelink, H. & Seeverens, T. (2001). We zitten op een breekpunt. *De Voetbaltrainer, 100,* 2-11.

Kormelink, H. & Seeverens, T. (2002). „Het gaat om 'het zien van' en specifieke kwaliteiten". *De Voetbaltrainer, 108,* 2-9.

Kormelink, H., Seeverens, T. & Adriaanse, C. (1993). Die High-Tech-Ausbildung von Ajax Amsterdam. Einblicke in das Talentförderungsmodell des niederländischen Rekordmeisters. *fußballtraining, 9,* 3-11.

Kraif, U. (Red.). (2007). *Duden. Das große Fremdwörterbuch.* Herkunft und Bedeutung der Fremdwörter. Mannheim: Dudenverlag.

Kröger, C. & Roth, K. (1999). *Ballschule. Ein ABC für Spielanfänger.* Schorndorf: Hofmann.

Kubierske, K. & Pabst, K. (2002). Austrias Ausbildungskonzept. *fußballtraining, 2,* 32-38.

Leerkes, J. (2003). Van Basten und Mühren lehren TIPS. *kicker, 66,* 56.

Lames, M., Augste, C., Dreckmann, C., Görsdorf, K. & Schimanski, M. (2008). Der „Relative Age Effect" (RAE): neue Hausaufgaben für den Sport. *Leistungssport, 6,* 4-9.

Lemmink, K. A. P. M., Verheijen, R. & Visscher, C. (2004). The discriminative power of the Interval Shuttle Run Test and the Maximal Multistage Shuttle Run Test for playing level of soccer. *Journal of Sports Medicine and Physical Fitness, 44* (3), 233-239.

Lutz, H. (2010). *Besser Fußball spielen mit Life Kinetik®*. München: BLV Buchverlag.

Mariman, H. (2002a). Functionele techniek bij de jongste voetballers. *De Voetbaltrainer, 103,* 20-30.

Mariman, H. (2002b). „Zeister visie en de Coerver-methode bijten elkaar niet". *De Voetbaltrainer, 109,* 31-39.
McShane, K. (2002). Youth soccer training at FC Barcelona. *Success in Soccer, 5,* 4-15.

Mechling, H. & Munzert, J. (Hrsg.). (2003). *Handbuch Bewegungswissenschaft-Bewegungslehre.* Schorndorf: Hofmann.
Memmert, D. (2006). *Optimales Taktiktraining im Leistungsfußball.* Band 1. Balingen: Spitta Verlag.

Memmert, D. & Roth, K. (2003). Individualtaktische Leistungsdiagnostik im Sportspiel. *Spectrum der Sportwissenschaften, 15,* 44-70.

Meyer, T. & Faude, O. (2006). Feldtests im Fußball. *Deutsche Zeitschrift für Sportmedizin, 57* (5), 147-148.

Michels, R. (2000a). *Teambuilding als route naar succes.* Leeuwarden: Eisma BV.

Michels, R. (2000b). Trainer müssen Visionen haben. *fußballtraining, 9,* 4-5.

Müllender, B. (2010). HUP Alemanija Hup. 11 Freunde. *Zugriff am 08. August 2010* unter www.11freunde.de/bundesligen131793hup_alemanija_hup.htm.

Neumaier, A. (1999). *Koordinatives Anforderungsprofil und Koordinationstraining.* Köln: Sport und Buch Strauß.

Neumann, G. (2009). *Talentdiagnose und Talentprognose im Nachwuchsleistungssport.* 2. BISP-Symposium: Theorie trifft Praxis. Bonn.

Pabst, K. (2001). Talentförderung: Wie machen es die anderen? Teil 7: Niederlande. *fußballtraining, 1,* 38-43.

Pfeiffer, M. (2010). *Das Problem Pause.* kicker, 62, 20-21.

Petersen, E. (2001). Vertrouwen is de basis om goed te kunnen samenwerken. *De Voetbaltrainer, 101,* 20-24.

Raab, M. (2001). *SMART: Techniken des Taktiktrainings – Taktiken des Techniktrainings.* Köln.

Reviersport. (2003). Schalke 04: Alles wie früher. *Reviersport – Fußball im Revier 2003/2004 – Extra Hinrunde, 31,* 125-126.

Roth, K. (2000). Die Straßenspielhypothese oder das Modell der inzidentiellen Inkubation – Ein Erklärungsansatz für die Kreativitätsentwicklung im Sportspiel. In W. Schmidt & A. Knollenberg (Hrsg.), *Sport-Spiel-Forschung: Gestern. Heute. Morgen* (S. 159-163). Hamburg: Czwalina.

Roth, K. (2005). D 2 Sportspiel-Vermittlung. In A. Hohmann, M. Kolb & K. Roth (Hrsg.), *Handbuch Sportspiel* (S. 290-308). Schorndorf: Hofmann.

Röser, U. (2010). Robin DUTT. *kicker, 62,* 28-29.

Röthig, P. (1992). *Sportwissenschaftliches Lexikon.* Schorndorf: Hofmann.

Ruiz, L. (2002). *The Spanish Soccer Coaching Bible. Volume 1 – Youth & Club.* Auburn, Michigan: Reedswain Publishing.

Rummenigge, K.-H. (1998). „An den runden Tisch gehört auch Udo Lattek". *Sport-Bild, 29,* 24.

Rutemöller, E. (2001). Coaching: Denksport für den Trainer. *fußballtraining, 11 + 12,* 6-9.

Schlieck, T. (2010). Mit dem Zweiten (Auge) hält man besser! *fußballtraining, 6 + 7,* 76-85.

Schlumberger, A. (2010). *Fitnesstraining bei den DFB-Junioren – Bewegungskoordination und -ökonomie als Basis des fußballspezifischen Fitnesstrainings.* Vortrag vom 29.4.2010 zur Fortbildungsveranstaltung des BDFL (Verbandsgruppe Westfalen) im SportCentrum Kaiserau.

Schreiner, P. (1997). Das Basistraining des FC Schalke 04. *fußballtraining, 6,* 38-39.

Schreiner, P. (1999). *Erfolgreich dribbeln. Das Peter-Schreiner-System.* Reinbek bei Hamburg: Rowohlt.

Schreiner, P. (2006). *FUSSBALL – Kinder- und Jugendtraining.* Reinbek bei Hamburg: Rowohlt.

Schreiner, P. (2009). *FUSSBALL – Perfekte Ballbeherrschung.* Aachen: Meyer & Meyer.

Schulze-Marmeling, D. (2010). *Barça oder: Die Kunst des schönen Spiels.* Göttingen: Verlag Die Werkstatt.

Seeger, F. (2008). *Coaching im Wettkampfsport. Eine empirische Untersuchung im Fußball.* Hamburg: Diplomica Verlag.

Seeverens, T. (1999). Het talent en zijn ouders. *De Voetbaltrainer, 81,* 56-58.

Seeverens, T. (2001a). In een paar jaar tijd ben ik een andere trainer geworden. *De Voetbaltrainer, 99,* 2-9.

Seeverens, T. (2001b). Techniektraining in relatie met positie en taken. *De Voetbaltrainer, 102*, 18-24.

SID (1998). Rijkaards Zukunft liegt im Südosten von Amsterdam. *Saarbrücker Zeitung, 268*, 13.

Smentek, K. & Salomon, B. (2010). „Deutsche Spieler haben mehr Leidenschaft". *kicker*, 64, 6-8

Smink, J. (2001). De leeftijdscategorie van „presteren met plezier". *De Voetbaltrainer, 97*, 36-41.

Smink, J. (2002). Koeman: „Passen en trappen is de basis". *Trainersmagazine, 1*, 20-21.

Smink, J. (2003). „Het is een proces dat langzaam gestalte krijgt". *Trainersmagazine, 2*, 20-21.

Sports. (1996). Ist der holländische Fußball besser als der Deutsche? *Sports, 4*, 1.

Sternberg, R. J. & Lubart, T. I. (1995). *Defying the crowd.* New York: Free Press.

Stiglbauer, R. (2010). *Spezielles Ausdauertraining im Fußballsport. High Intensity Training in Form von Kleinfeldspielen zur Entwicklung der maximalen Sauerstoffaufnahme.* Saarbrücken: VDM Verlag Dr. Müller.

Stöber, B. & Peter, R. (2003). Vorbereitung auf das 4-3-3-System. *fußballtraining, 4*, 22-29.

Stoop, T. (1999). Een project voor kinderen uit achterstandswijken. *De Voetbaltrainer, 83*, 57-59.

Stoop, T. (2001). Meer kwaliteit aan de basis. *De Voetbaltrainer, 100*, 38-44.

Tamboer, J. (1979). Sich Bewegen – ein Dialog zwischen Mensch und Welt. *Sportpädagogik, 3* (2), 14-19.

ten Hag, E. (2010, April). *Training der Fußballkondition.* Vortrag vom 29.4.2010 zur Fortbildungsveranstaltung des BDFL (Verbandsgruppe Westfalen) im SportCentrum Kaiserau.

te Poel, H.-D. (1987). Aufwärmen – komplex und funktionell. *fußballtraining, 5* (10), 3-9.

te Poel, H-D. & Eisfeld, H. (1987). Verbesserung der Schnelligkeit im Fußball. 1. Teil: Vorbemerkungen und Trainingseinheit zur Verbesserung der Koordination. *fußballtraining, 5* (11), 3-10.

te Poel, H.-D. (1995a). Nachwuchstraining im Fußball. Teil 1: Theorie und Praxis des Trainings der Technikvariationen und der taktischen Fähigkeiten und Fertigkeiten. *Lehrhilfen für den Sportunterricht, 44* (7), 102-107.

te Poel, H.-D. (1995b). Nachwuchstraining im Fußball. Teil 2: Spiel- und Übungsformen zur Theorie und Praxis des Technikvariationstrainings (TV) und der taktischen Fähigkeiten (TFÄ) und Fertigkeiten (TFE) im Angriffsspiel. *Lehrhilfen für den Sportunterricht, 44* (8), 122-128.

te Poel, H.-D. (2002). „Nachwuchsförderung im Fußballsport – Neue Wege in Deutschland und Europa". Bericht über die 17. Jahrestagung der dvs-Kommission Fußball. *dvs-Informationen, 17* (2), 46-49.

te Poel, H.-D. (2009). Buchbesprechung: Memmert, D. (2006). Optimales Taktiktraining im Leistungsfußball. *Spectrum der Sportwissenschaften, 21* (2), 83-88.

Thumfart, M. (2006). *Optimales Taktiktraining im Jugendfußball.* Band 2. Balingen: Spitta Verlag.

Tomaz, C. (2007). *Spielsystem von Morgen effektiv trainieren. Fußballtaktik Band 1.* Duisburg.

Trosse, H.-D. (2000). *Der erfolgreiche Trainer: Führung – Motivation – Psychologie.* Aachen: Meyer & Meyer.

Universitair Centrum Pro Motion Groningen. (2009). *Intervall Shuttle Run Test (ISRT).* Leer.

van Barneveld, H. & Vervoorm, C. (1997). *Handleiding Talentontwikkeling.* Arnhem: NOC+NSF.

van den Brande, F. (2002). „We komen fysiek te kort". *Trainersmagazine, 1,* 26-29.

van der Meer, F. (2000). *Op weg naar 4 tegen 4.* 2. Aufl. Zeist: KNVB.

van Gaal, Louis. (2006). De doelstelling creeert de oefenvorm. Slender, H. & van Veen, P. *Trainersmagazine, 5,* 4-13.

van Gaal, Louis. (2010a, Januar). Abendzeitung.de. Zugriff am 9.1.2010 unter www.abendzeitung.de/Sport/fc-bayern/157662

van Gaal, Louis. (2010b). *Biografie & Visie.* Publish Unlimited.

van Lingen, B. (2001). *Coachen van jeugdvoetballers.* Zeist: KNVB.

van Lingen, B. & Pauw, V. (2001a). *De bal is rond . . . en dat is best moeilijk.* Zeist: KNVB.

van Lingen, B. & Pauw, V. (2001b). *Techniek in Voetballen.* Zeist: KNVB.

van Loon, J., van Lingen, B., Pauw, V. & Dokter, R. (1998). Scouting voor het jeugdplan Nederland. *De Voetbaltrainer, 78,* 32-40.

van't Haar, P. (1999a). De eeuwige zoektocht naar hét talent. *De Voetbaltrainer, 81,* 43-46.

van't Haar, P. (1999b). „Zorg dat talent vooral plezier in voetballen houdt". *De Voetbaltrainer, 81,* 59-65.

van Veen, P. (2003). Voetballers opleiden is mensen opleiden! *Trainersmagazine, 5*, 16-21.

van Veen, P. & Smink, J. (2003). Tweebenigheid is het belangrijkst bij F-jes Ajax. *Trainersmagazine, 1*, 36-39.

Verheijen, R. (1997). *Handboek Voetbalconditie.* Leeuwarden: Eisma bv.

Verheijen, R. (1999/2000). *Handbuch Fußballkondition.* Leer: bfp Versand Anton Lindemann.

Verheijen, R. (2009a). Warum die Russen so fit waren. *fußballtraining, 27* (1 + 2), 26-32.

Verheijen, R. (2009b). Trainieren Sie traditionell oder richtig? *fußballtraining, 27* (10), 6-14.

Vieth, N. (1995). Mit Nachwuchsarbeit zum Europacup-Titel. *fußballtraining, 5 + 6*, 23-31.

Vitesse Arnhem. (2002). *Vitesse Voetbal Academie.* Arnhem: Vitesse Arnhem.

Voetbal Academie Sparta Rotterdam. (2002). *Techniek – Snelheid – Zelfvertrouwen.* Rotterdam: Voetbalacademie.

Wein, H. (2001). *Developing youth soccer players.* Windsor: Human Kinectics.

Wein, H. (2004). *Entwicklung der Spielintelligenz im Fußball.* Heinsberg.

Weineck, J. (2007). *Optimales Training unter besonderer Berücksichtigung des Kinder- und Jugendtrainings.* Balingen: Spitta Verlag.

Werthner, R. (2001). Sportmotorische Leistungsdiagnostik als Grundlage für Selektionsentscheidungen bzw. eine prognostisch orientierte „Talent"-Förderung im Fußball. *Österreichisches Journal für Sportmedizin, 31* (2), 6-12.

Winner, D. (2008). *Oranje brillant. Das neurotische Genie des holländischen Fußballs.* Köln: Verlag Kiepenheuer & Witsch.

Interviews

Interview with Danny Blind: 2003 Youth Coordinator of Dutch Record Champions Ajax Amsterdam. Conducted on May 8, 2003 in Amsterdam, the Netherlands.

Interview with Harry Dost: running and conditioning coach for youth and professional players at Dutch first division club and 2010 Dutch Champions Twente Enschede. Conducted on March 31, 2003 in Duisburg-Wedau, Germany.

Interview with René Hake: Head Junior Coach and U23 Coach at 2010 Dutch Champions Twente Enschede. Conducted on Jan. 12, 2010 in Enschede, the Netherlands.

Interview with Henk Heising: Youth Coordinator and Assistant Coach of the Professional team of Dutch national league club SC Heerenveen. Conducted on May 20, 2003 in Heerenveen, the Netherlands.

Interview with Cliff McDonald: Coerver Coach at Soccer Academy of Sparta Rotterdam. Conducted on Feb. 23, 2003 in Rotterdam, the Netherlands.

Written interview with Olde Riekerink: Youth coordinator at Ajax Amsterdam. Conducted from March 17, 2010.

Interview with René Meulensteen: First Team Coach at Manchester United. Conducted on Feb. 12, 2010.

Interview with Nico Romeijn: Head Coach at the KNVB and Member of the UEFA Coaches Forum. Conducted on Feb. 10, 2010 in Zeist.

Interview with Iddo Roscher: Youth coordinator at Dutch national league club NEC Nijmegen. Conducted on Feb. 10, 2000 in Nijmegen.

Two interviews with Thomas Schlieck: Goalkeeping coach for youth and professional players at German second division club DCS Arminia Bielefeld and holder of the Dutch Goalkeeping Coach's Diploma according to the "Frans Hoek Method." Conducted on May 22, 2002 in Bielefeld, Germany.

Interview with Huub Stevens: 18-time Dutch national player, player at Fortuna Sittard and PSV Eindhoven and soccer coach at PSV Eindhoven (juniors and seniors), Roder Kerkrade, Schalke 04, Hertha BSC Berlin, 1. FC Cologne, Hamburger SV and 2010 Austrian champion with Red Bull Salzburg. Conducted on Jan. 19, 2010.

Interview with Edward Sturing: 2003 youth coordinator at Dutch first division club Vitesse Arnhem and then Head Coach of the professional team at Vitesse. Conducted on March 13, 2003 in Arnhem, the Netherlands.

Interview with Peter van Amstel: Association Coach at KNVB East District. Conducted on Jan. 28, 2003 in Deventer, the Netherlands.

Interview with Ed van Lingen: 2003 Manager of the Soccer Academy of Sparta Rotterdam. Conducted on Feb. 23, 2003 in Rotterdam, the Netherlands.

Interview with Fons van den Brande: Former conditioning coach at Dutch first division club Vitesse Arnhem and for nine years conditioning coach in the Papendal National Sports Center. In 1996, he founded the company *sportpartners*. Conducted on Feb. 10, 2010 in Velp, the Netherlands.

Interview with Paul van Veen: Editor in Chief of the internationally renowned Dutch Coach's review trainersmagazine on the state of development of youth soccer in the Netherlands and Germany. Conducted on Dec. 14, 2009 in Zeist, the Netherlands.

Interview with Horst Wein: youth coach at the Center for Development and Research at the Royal Spanish Soccer Federation (CEDIF) and coach at Nike Great Britain for the "Premier Football Training Program". Conducted on May 4, 2003 in Duisburg-Wedau, Germany.

Photo Credits

Jacket Design: Sabine Groten

Jacket photos: Imago Sportfotodienst GmbH;
© Yuriy Panyukov/Hemera/Thinkstock;
© Matt Knannlein/iStockphoto/Thinkstock;
© Todd Arena/Hemera/Thinkstock

Interior photos: Paul van Veen, Chief Editor of Soccer Coaching International, Beatrixlaan 21, 2811 LZ Reeuwijk, The Netherlands

Graphics: David Siebers; Software: easysports graphics

Demonstration "Pull through Turn" and "Pull Spin"
Jens te Poel (DFB high performance center player)

Peter Schreiner
SOCCER – PERFECT BALL CONTROL

Want to learn how to dribble and feint like Maradona or Ronaldinho, and to juggle the ball like Jay-Jay Okocha or Edgar Davids? In this book, players learn how to become good ball handlers and master tricks that enable them to score more goals while playing attractive, offensive soccer.

2nd edition
208 p., full-color print, 205 photos, 134 illus.
Paperback, 6 ^{1}/2" x 9 ^{1}/4"
ISBN: 9781841262789
E-Book: 9781841265728
$ 16.95 US/$ 29.95 AUS/£ 12.95 UK/€ 16.95

Gerhard Frank
SOCCER TRAINING PROGRAMS

Success on the soccer field demands a high degree of fitness, technical skill and tactical ability. This book offers amateur coaches training programs that meet these requirements while remaining safe, interesting and fun. The programs have been adapted specifically for the amateur game.

2nd edition, 216 p., full-color print, 74 photos, 15 Illus., 96 training programs, Paperback, 6 ^{1}/2" x 9 ^{1}/4"
ISBN: 9781841262741
E-Book: 9781841265742
$ 17.95 US/$ 29.95 AUS/£ 12.95 UK/€ 16.95

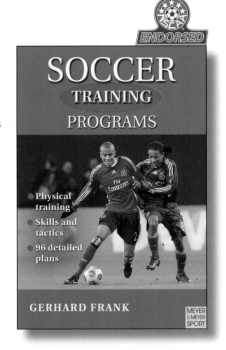

All books available as **mediaTresor** E-books.
SECURE E-BOOK
Secure & user-friendly

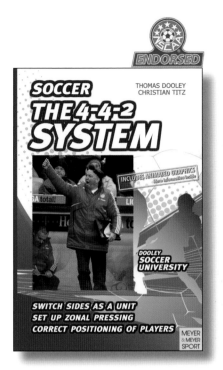
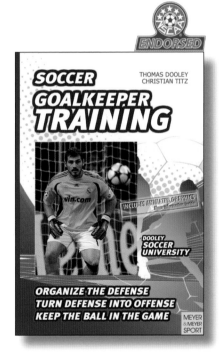